Mission Statement

This is an initiative of the Tamil Nadu Textbook and Educational Services Corporation (TNTB & ESC) under the aegis of one of the announcements for the year 2021-22, titled 'Thisaidhorum Dravidam' by Honourable Minister for School Education Thiru Anbil Mahesh Poyyamozhi to identify and translate into English, Kannada, Malayalam and Telugu, Tamil literary works, that they might enhance the reach of Tamil antiquity, tradition and contemporaneity and enrich world literature and to also translate significant literary voices from other Dravidian languages into Tamil. Both ventures are to be undertaken as either independent or joint publications with collaborating publishers.

The Life and Work of Moovalur Ramamirtham Ammaiyar

The Life and Work of Moovalur Ramamirtham Ammaiyar

B JEEVASUNDARI

Translated from Tamil by
V BHARATHI HARISHANKAR

zubaan

zubaan

ZUBAAN
128 B Shahpur Jat, 1st floor
NEW DELHI 110 049
Email: contact@zubaanbooks.com
Website: www.zubaanbooks.com

First published by Zubaan Publishers Pvt. Ltd 2024

10 9 8 7 6 5 4 3 2 1

ISBN 978 93 90514 97 7 (paperback)
ISBN 978 93 90514 67 0 (hardback)
ISBN 978 93 90514 86 1 (ebook)

Zubaan is an independent feminist publishing house based in New Delhi with a strong academic and general list. It was set up as an imprint of India's first feminist publishing house, Kali for Women, and carries forward Kali's tradition of publishing world quality books to high editorial and production standards. *Zubaan* means tongue, voice, language, speech in Hindustani. Zubaan publishes in the areas of the humanities, social sciences, as well as in fiction, general non-fiction, and books for children and young adults under its Young Zubaan imprint.

Typeset by in Bell MT Std 11/13 by Jojy Philip
Printed and bound at Thomson Press India Ltd

Contents

Annexures

Preface to the First Edition
A Fragment from Tamil History

'I don't know about Moovalur to the same extent that I know about the Steppes, the Siberian snowscape, the Kyrgyzian forests, the Ural and the Alps mountains.'

The readers who read the above statement should not mistake me for a globe trotter, who has missed the opportunity to know about Moovalur. I was born and brought up in Mayiladuthurai. I have also lived for three years in Moovalur, where Ramamirtham Ammaiyar lived. Our home was in the locality near 'Shop Chellappa,' (now known as 'Chella Stores'), which was owned by her son, Chellappa. Even so, I do not know about Moovalur Ramamirtham Ammaiyar to the extent I know about Russia and Russian literature. We make it a point to know about Russia. We are eager to get information about America. I cited the above example just to point out our apathy and neglect of our own history. It's another matter that there has been no publication about the life of Moovalur Ramamirtham Ammaiyar.

Even though I was born and raised in Mayiladuthurai, I first heard about Moovalur Ramamirtham Ammaiyar only in 1984. Around this time, there was a public meeting in Moovalur. The then propaganda secretary of All India Anna Dravida Munnetra

Kazhagam (AIADMK), Jayalalitha, addressed the gathering. Before beginning her speech, she pointed to a house opposite and stated: 'I deem it a privilege to address the gathering in front of the house and in the town, where Moovalurar, the braveheart who fought for the abolition of the devadasi system lived.' This was the very first information that I received about Moovalurar.

This was followed by the publication of an excerpt from Moovalurar's novel, *Dasigalin Mosa Valai* or *Mathi Petra Minor*, in the annual literary issue of *India Today* under the category of Dravidian Literature. That excerpt and the details given about her whetted my curiosity to know more. It was only after this reading that I started searching for more details about her. However, I did not find much information. It was a shock and a surprise for me that I could not get information about a well-known social reformer.

Even when the issue of the abolition of the devadasi system is discussed, there is no mention of Moovalurar who dedicated her entire life to the cause. I decided I wanted to know more about her life and my search began. I became aware that a lot of information about her remains hidden even now. I understood that the books on Tamil history have completely neglected Moovalurar. And we complain about English books ignoring Tamil Nadu! How do we, who make such complaints, act? We follow the entrenched caste hierarchy. We neglect those born in the lower caste and who fought for the uplift of the downtrodden even while writing their history. We reluctantly accept those who were born in the oppressed groups only when they fight the odds and reach a respectable position in society. The case in point is Muthulakshmi Reddy. However, we acknowledge and mention Moovalurar even less than Muthulakshmi Reddy. I decided to write a complete historical work on Moovalurar based on the information collected from different sources.

In 2003, I applied to the Sahitya Akademi, to publish a book on Moovalurar as part of the series on 'Makers of Indian Literature.' Whatever the reason, I am yet to receive a reply from them. I decided to carry forward the publication on my own. After this, my search began in earnest. First, I tried and collected the essays about her as well as her writings. I was able to find information only in magazines of the Dravidian movement. I did not find information about her in any other common magazines or journals. I cannot say that I found a lot of information about her life and work in Dravidian magazines. Only the few essays, which appeared during the life time of Moovalurar, provide some information about her life. These details were insufficient to document the life of a person, who had contributed to public life for over five decades. Hence, I undertook field-based research in Mayiladuthurai and Moovalur.

Despite the fact that Moovalurar spent a major part of her life in Mayiladuthurai and Moovalur, people who had known her, including the followers of the Dravidian movement, were not willing to share information. It was both disappointing and shocking for me. I met her relatives and people who had taken part along with her in social reform activities. Her so-called relatives were unwilling to reveal their caste identity. These were some of the problems in writing about recent history.

These may have been the reasons why I had not heard about her. The first place where I could find information was the library of Anna Arivalayam. The librarian, Sundararajan, has extensive knowledge on the Dravidian movement. He collected the details on Moovalurar and also permitted me to photocopy them. I was able to plan the structure of my book based on this information.

I am indebted to many people for the completion of the book. First and foremost, my gratitude goes to my father,

Late Comrade Cuddalore Balan. From a very young age, he introduced me to good books. He helped me build my thoughts in the world of books. The primary reason for my independent nature is his affection and support. At this juncture, I remember and thank him for his support in publishing this book. Next in the list is the intellectual doyen, Comrade Chinna Kuthoosi. He was a father figure and mentor who taught me not only the importance of the Dravidian movement but also the basic premises and tenets of life. He continued to encourage me in the course of writing this book. In addition, he has also written the foreword to the book. Even though he does not encourage such formalities, I cannot but thank him. Thirdly, I would like to thank my dear friend and teacher, R Jawahar. For many years, he has encouraged me to write about the history of the Tamils. It is another matter that I have still not started writing about the history of Tamil Nadu. The present volume is but a fragment of that history.

My dear friend Amarantha always strives to work with a larger social perspective in spite of the bitterness that pervades life. She also enthuses me to work in a similar manner. From the time I started writing this book, she has shown more interest in it than me. My affectionate thanks to her. Next, I would like to thank Selvaraj, Moovalurar's grandson. He acted as the touchstone to verify the authenticity of the details that I had gathered. He had remained with Moovalurar during the last 30 years of her life. He is the only living person who has first-hand knowledge about Moovalurar, and who grew up surrounded by her love and care. He has not only adopted but has also followed her principles. At present [at the time of writing], he is 74 years old. It was a heartwarming moment when he shared his experiences with Moovalurar during an interview. He also shared some of her rare photographs.

In this book, I have mentioned several times the term '*My Life History:* handwritten manuscript.' The document is incomplete and further, the year of composition has not been recorded anywhere. I could get only 15 pages of what was written in a notebook. Moovalurar has mentioned in that manuscript that she started writing her autobiography on the behest and encouragement of N S Krishnan and K A Thangavelu.

The same manuscript has been suitably edited and published as *My Life* in a serialised form in the *Annai* magazine published by Sathyavani Muthu. Copies of all the issues could not be found. This handwritten manuscript was given to me by Moovalurar's great granddaughter. She was not keen on revealing any details about herself. Many thanks to her for giving me the invaluable manuscript.

My thanks to my husband, Comrade M Appanasamy, for translating the relevant parts of the 'Prohibition of Dedication (of Devadasi) Act.' Further thanks to brother Konangi for lending me the book, *Thiru Vi Ka: Notes on His Life,* and letting me keep it for a long time. My dear brother Jeevamani for designing the cover and the layout of the book [the first edition] so well. Even though it feels like cliché, thanks to all of them.

Thanks to Comrade Siva Senthilnathan of *Matru Pathippagam* for putting up with my missed deadlines for over a year. Sincere thanks to all the friends in the publication house. Further thanks to retired teacher from Mayiladuthurai, Sittharkadu Meenakshisundaram for sharing valuable inputs, Moovalur Arumugham Chettiar, 'Chella Stores' Kaliyamurthy, Meenambal Vellaithambi, S Balakrishnan, librarian of Melpathy Thiru Vi Ka library, former friends from the Dravida Kazhagam, Mayilduthurai Sundaram and 'Pappa' Arunachalam.

This book has attempted to present information about Moovalurar's life and work. It may have some mistakes and need some corrections. If readers and scholars can give their valuable comments, it will help in revising the next edition.

B Jeevasundari
Ambattur, Chennai, 2006

Preface to the Second Edition

Books travel through time. No matter how dog-eared a book's pages become after constant use, if it is a good book, it renews itself. A book speaks to its readers. A book awaits a male or a female reader across generations. It struggles against the ravages of time. As a reader, that was my belief—that every book waited for its time.

At this juncture, when the second edition of my own book is being published, I am duty bound to thank the books I have read. I am able to understand the need for a second edition because of the enthusiasm shown by many publishers to bring it out eight years after the publication of the first edition of this book. The need for another edition has arisen out of the responsibility to make the book reach more people at a time when fundamentalist forces are rearing their ugly heads. Ayya Chinna Kuthoosi, who constantly encouraged me to write the book and who wrote a foreword to the first edition, is no more. Had he been alive, he would have been very happy.

Now, I would like to document the context of Tamil publishing, readership and research background which would be useful for those who wish to continue the conversations on these issues which also inform and highlight a few important aspects of my first book.

First of all, my heartfelt gratitude to the reviews and criticisms on the book, which have helped spread Moovalur Ramamirtham Ammaiyar's life and works to many people. It should have happened much earlier. The 'better late than never' attitude adopted by the followers of the Dravidian movement, the socialist movement and the women's liberation movement, as well as the felicitations and welcome accorded to the book are really meant for Moovalurar. I am happy to have helped bring her work to life.

I would like to speak here of the psychology of caste. After reading the book, many people who did not know me personally, called and expressed their appreciation. But along with the praise, there was a question too: 'Are you a relative of Moovalur Ammaiyar?' Their curiosity was because they wanted to find out if I belonged to the same caste. My response was, 'Can I write about Ammaiyar only if I belong to her caste? Isn't her work for society at large? Can't anyone write about the life of a woman who fought against the social degradation that had persisted for over two thousand years?' My responses were present in these questions and this silenced the persons who interrogated my intentions. However, what lay behind these questions was nauseating. It is puzzling to note that the umbilical cord of caste, perpetrated by patriarchal lineage, was broken by the tireless efforts and lifelong struggles of a braveheart who set aside caste and religion, but sadly, she is still not understood. We need to ponder whether this should continue in the 21st century as well. My feeling is that such questions would not have been raised if I had not been a woman.

Despite this kind of prejudice, it is good to note that this book has reached the younger generation. In particular, many women have been attracted to it, and some have decided to work on Moovalurar for their doctoral degrees and have approached me for guidance. Tragically, their supervisors have cited this book as the only available resource and have refused to grant permission. A young man from Hyderabad approached me (and also met me in person) and told me that he planned to work on Moovalurar. I provided a lot of information and advice. For form's sake, he jotted down the details I gave. When he was about to leave, he requested: 'Please hand over all the source information, notes, archival documents and photographs gathered over many years in your search for Ammaiyar's history. I can then finish my PhD.' He made this request without any embarrassment or guilt. It took a long time for me to get over the shock of his demand, but this is how it works these days.

More interesting is my struggle to obtain library orders for the book. I didn't write the book for profit. I wanted it to be in important libraries. My desire was to see it being read for a long time to come. That is why I wanted to apply and receive permission from the Library Scrutiny Committee. I am glad I was successful in obtaining their approval.

Even though there are a few concerns like these, a lesson on Moovalurar's life has been included in the Tamil Nadu Government's Samacheer Kalvi Thittam's textbook, first published in 2010 and still in use. That the present book was the basis for that lesson is heart-warming. Even more touching is the fact that a Tamil teacher in Bengaluru has read the book and recommended it to be included in the Karnataka Government syllabus for Tamil education. At present, Moovalurar's life has been written as a lesson for students in Karnataka, another touching instance.

In Tamil Nadu, the only person who can fill the vacuum created by the demise of Ayya Chinna Kuthoosi is the Dravidian movement scholar Thiru K Thirunavukkarasu. He is a veritable storehouse of Dravidian thought and has been encouraging me to write over a long period. I wanted him to write the foreword to the second edition. When I approached him, readily agreed and wrote a brilliant foreword. My sincere thanks to him.

At the time when I also approached Anandhi, who has researched extensively on women in the movement and on feminism, for another foreword. Tragically, her husband, M S S Pandian, had just passed away. Even in that hour of grief, she did not refuse my request. Not only did she write an excellent foreword but also came home in person to hand it over. I cannot forget that simplicity and camaraderie.

Finally, I also want to share my sense of guilt for not writing a few books in the interim period as a token of gratitude for the reach of the first edition. What is to be done? Health issues and life itself pulls us in the opposite direction. We win sometimes and we lose many times. Amidst this struggle is the hope that I will succeed in the future.

I also remember with gratitude my father who introduced me to literature and politics at an early age. I recall with thanks the constant learning experiences given to me by Ayya Chinna Kuthoosi and the benevolent, fatherly presence of Comrade R Jawahar. It is not a mere formality to thank my dear friend and husband Appanasamy, who always provides constructive suggestions and support to my work. My affectionate thanks to my sibling Jeevamani who designed the cover and illustrations for the first edition and Comrade Nagarajan who came forward to publish this book through Bharathi Puthakalayam.

B Jeevasundari
Chennai, 2016

Preface to the English Translation

'The major drawback of the early phase of the Dravidian movement is that it did not pay attention or show interest to write and record the lives of its prominent leaders.'

'Once, Medappa, the Judge of Karnataka High Court asked Arignar Annadurai for a book on the history of the Dravidian movement. Anna was unable to fulfil his request. That kind of a lacuna has continued for a long time.' These are the words of the doyen of the Dravidian Movement, a senior journalist and a storehouse of knowledge, Thiru. Chinna Kuthoosi (Thiruvarur Thiagarasan), who has written the Foreword to the present volume.

The first complete historical documentation of Moovalur Ramamirtham Ammaiyar's life appeared in 2006, around 43 years after her death. It was entitled, *Moovalur Ramamirtham: Vazhvum Paniyum* in Tamil. Prior to this publication, since the 1950s, only a handful of essays had appeared in magazines about the Dravidian movement. The focus of those essays was on Moovalurar's socio-political contributions to the Congress party, the Self-Respect Movement, the Dravidar Kazhagam and Dravida Munnetra Kazhagam parties. In particular, many of the articles discussed her role in the anti-Hindi agitation. Very few looked at her efforts to abolish the devadasi system. Nor did they discuss her lifelong struggle and her contributions to the formation of the Nagapasathar Sangam, which was later renamed as the Isai Vellala Sangam. The bitter truth is that even now, there are very few discussions about her life and contributions to society. And there is almost a complete silence about her service to the abolishing of the devadasi system.

During Kalaignar Karunanidhi's tenure in 1989, a Marriage Assistance Scheme of ₹5000 named after Moovalurar provided monetary help to girls who had completed the eighth grade. After that, through successive tenures of different governments, the scheme was continued and the amount was enhanced. From September 2022, the scheme has taken a different form and has been elevated to a higher level. Girls who have completed their school education from the sixth to the twelfth grade in government schools, are provided ₹1000 as scholarship to fulfil their aspirations for higher education under the Pudhumai Penn Thittam in the name of Moovalurar. This effort is truly praiseworthy. The Marriage Assistance Scheme has been transformed into an Educational Assistance Scheme to provide continued access to higher education for girls. Once girls are provided an education, they can become self-reliant and take care of their marriage, family and future. They will be able to face whatever odds life may throw at them independently and with courage. For women, this is a welcome move to aid their development. That this scheme has been launched in the name of Moovalurar is laudable.

One major reason why the contributions of social reformers go unnoticed in the world at large is because of the lack of translations. In particular, if their works are translated into English, they reach a wider audience and there is scope for further translations into foreign languages. Even though, many scholars have emphasized the need to foreground Moovalurar's life and works through translation, suitable avenues did not open up. When I approached possible translators, it seemed the time was not right for them. It is unfortunate that there was a long gap in finding a suitable translator, even though the Tamil original was published in 2006.

During the COVID lockdown, my desire to get this book translated into English was rekindled. I spoke about the book to the Tamil Nadu Textbook and Educational Services Corporation since they were involved in translations of several books. The then AIADMK government did not pay much heed to the effort. I reminded the Tamil Nadu Textbook and Educational Services Corporation about the book when the Dravida Munnetra Kazhagam formed the government. They accepted my request immediately. After that, Dr V Bharathi Harishankar, Professor of English at the University of Madras took on the translation. Soon after the work began, she had to move to Coimbatore to assume charge as the Vice Chancellor of Avinashilingam Institute for Home Science and Higher Education for Women (Deemed University) and this delayed the translation. Despite her hectic schedule, she has translated the book very well. My heartfelt thanks to her.

After such a long journey, the Tamil Nadu Textbook and Educational Services Corporation has undertaken to move the translation work forward in a remarkable manner. My sincere gratitude to them. These are not empty words uttered for the sake of formality but reflect my emotions and feelings. Affectionate thanks to Zubaan, the feminist publisher, who have come forward to publish this book along with the Tamil Nadu Textbook and Educational Services Corporation.

That a moving force and a great personality like Moovalurar will be known and her contributions will be remembered across India through this translation is a matter of pride and joy.

B Jeevasundari
Chennai, 2023

Moovalurar – Poonkothai

A Stepping Stone

Foreword to the First Edition

Anyone who traces the history of the Dravidian movement and writes about the leaders who worked with Periyar cannot but place Moovalur Ramamirtham Ammaiyar at the top of the list. She worked with him when he was in the Congress party and staunchly supported him in his activities. When Periyar decided to leave the Congress party, she announced her decision and left as well. When Periyar started the Self-Respect Movement, she joined him and spearheaded the attempts to spread his ideology among people, especially women. In this manner, she dedicated her entire life and worked tirelessly for the movement and to dispel the superstitions that plagued people.

Leaders like Sir P T Thyagarayar, T M Nair and Dr Natesan started the Dravidian movement. Thanthai Periyar transformed it into a social reform movement to erase casteist oppression, to educate the people and make them knowledgeable and full of self-respect. He changed the movement into one that promoted rationalist thought.

Anna propagated Periyar's ideals among the youth, especially college goers, and converted the Dravidian movement into a political movement. Kalaignar proved through his exemplary leadership that the ideals of Periyar and Anna can be fulfilled by the democratically-elected government and that their dreams can be made real. In this list, Moovalurar has the distinction of enlightening the illiterate women who were enslaved by society, oppressed and treated like a child-bearing machines. She kindled the belief among women that they were not slaves. She was not only a propagandist but followed those ideals in her own life like a true braveheart.

Moovalurar fought to break the shackles that bound the body of women in the name of religion. Such women were assigned the identity of devadasis who were dedicated to temples but became the concubines of affluent landlords and priests for thousands of years. She was the *sutradhari* who worked behind the scenes to enable the enactment of law to prevent the devadasi system. In the dark era, when women could not venture out of the house, she was born into a devadasi family and raised by a devadasi but bravely entered politics. She campaigned shoulder to shoulder with men and participated in protests. She created history but her life history has not been documented in any form. The major criticism against the early years of the Dravidian movement was that no one showed interest in writing the life history of its prominent leaders. Once Medappa, a Judge of the Karnataka High Court, asked Anna to give him a book on the Dravidian movement so that he could understand the details but Anna could not find such a book.

This lacuna has existed for a long time. That there has been no historical work on the life of Moovalurar has been a strongly felt need. Jeevasundari has come forward to fill the gap through this slim volume. Even though the book is not exhaustive, she has tried her best to find resources and visited places where Moovalurar lived. She has struggled and succeeded in meeting Moovalurar's family and acquaintances to bring out her complete history. Her hard work shines in every page.

Jeevasundari belongs to a family who have followed socialist ideals. From her school days, she has been a voracious reader. She has written numerous essays on women's rights when she worked for little magazines such as *Puthiya Parvai*, *Penne Nee* and e-journals like *Aaraam Thinai*. That experience helped her write this book. The success of this book lies in its simple style of language, its sensitive use of words that do not scare away the readers and its total lack of ostentatious embellishments.

Whoever reads the book will not be satisfied but eager to know the complete life story of Moovalurar. This book will be a stepping stone for anyone who wants to collect more information and come forward to write a more comprehensive life history of Moovalurar. If this author undertakes that task, the book will reach far and wide.

There is no doubt that people who read this book will wholeheartedly wish and bless Jeevasundari so she may produce useful books like this.

Chinna Kuthoosi
Chennai, 2006

Foreword to the Second Edition

I read B Jeevasundari's book on Moovalur Ramamirtham Ammaiyar's life and works. The first edition was published by Arivai publications. The name *arivai* has several connotations including knowledge, intellect and intelligence. With the limited evidence that was available, Jeevasundari has presented a good book to the Tamil world. Her hard work shows in the quality of the book. The protagonist of this work, Moovalurar was a braveheart. Jeevasundari has painted a comprehensive picture of this individual, who was lost in the whirlwind of history. She has done this using stray pieces of evidence and disparate hidden lines.

Moovalurar was a compatriot of leaders like Gandhi Adigal, Periyar, Thiru Vi Ka, Varadajulu Naidu, Azhagar Samy and Arignar Anna. She worked in the same public arena and fought for social reform. Her greatest contribution was the fieldwork she did to contest the institutionalized practice of the devadasi system and her relentless battle to abolish it. This ritual of dedicating women has been practised in different parts of the world and it has also been recorded in the annals of the history of Tamil Nadu from time immemorial.

The Tamil people have always set great store by the virtue of chastity. Despite this, there has been a number of references to *parathaiyar*, that is, courtesans and prostitutes. The *Agam** literature presents these public women under different tropes such as: relationship with courtesans, the fight between the hero and heroine when the former returns from the house of the prostitute. A literary work even describes how royal elephants skidded and fell while stamping on the sandalwood paste which the man cast off on the grass after copulation with a prostitute. Indeed, there are no poets in Agam literature who do not refer to parathaiyar. Sangam literature talks about *varai ara magalir* or handmaidens, while *Thirukkural* refers to them as *varaivin magalir,* or women involved in sex work and prostitution. Marxist scholar Jothiprakasam, who wrote extensively on Sangam literature,* presents a new perspective on *marutham*, one of the eco types in the *thinai*† classification of Tholkkappiar, thus: 'The public women who peopled and dominated the ecotype of cultivable land present a lifestyle that broke free from the restrictions of family for the sake of love, thus creating a revolution.'

Even though this radicalization of relationships has been questioned and set aside as unwanted, it has developed and remained an integral part of the social structure. This was an

---

* Sangam literature can be broadly divided into Agam and Puram. While the former refers to tales of love and family, the latter deals with tales of war and courage.

† One of the five eco types mentioned in the thinai classification of land forms in Tamil culture and literature. It refers to cultivable land and its associated flora, fauna, and so on. The five-fold classification of land forms in Sangam literature includes a *kurinji* or mountainous region, *mullai* or pastoral region, *marutham* or wet agricultural land, *neythal* or coastal region and *palai* or desert region. These land forms not only have well-delineated flora, fauna, local cultural practices but evoke a specific emotion in the characters and connote a specific theme.

unwanted outcome of monarchy and feudalism. We cannot ignore or neglect the origin and development of this practice and the later acceptance of it as a mark of civilization. Due to constant wars between kingdoms, the male population decreased and the number of females increased. The surplus women were traditionally accepted as the wives and concubines of kings and this practice was exalted as the duty of a king. The rich and mighty followed the path of the king and laid claim to the women captured in war. This situation was not unique to Tamil Nadu.

The class of public women was formed by women orphaned during wars. Their numbers increased, thanks to the men who 'patronised' them. Different names were used in our literature to represent them. These include the following:

- *Uruthira kanigaiyar (dedicated to Siva temple)*
- *Kanigaiyar (Dedicated to any temple)*
- *Kamakizhathi (Not a wife but belongs to one man)*
- *Varaivin magalir (Equivalent of call girls in the present context)*
- *Kadhal parathaiyar (Concubine, who is the daughter of cheri parathaiyar)*
- *Il parathaiyar (One who was provided a place to stay and whose needs were taken care of by a man)*
- *Cheri parathaiyar (One who lived outside the main town and belonged to everyone)*
- *Devaradiyar (Literally translated as handmaiden of God, devadasis who were dedicated to gods and temples)*
- *Podhu magal (An umbrella term to refer to all the above).*

When a married couple was childless, it was a common practice for a man to remarry. This practice has been followed since the times of Tholkkapiyar. *Tholkkapiyam* refers to this type of marriage as 'the wedding to continue the lineage or family line.' If a man married twice in this manner and also took another woman, she was called *kamakizhathi*. The increasing numbers of destitute women arising out of social exigencies led them to learn dance and music and provide sexual comfort in return for money. Thiruvalluvar terms this group of women as *varaivin magalir*. The women who offered themselves for the love of one man were eulogized as *kadhal prathaiyar.* If such women were provided boarding, lodging and patronage, they were called *il parathaiyar*. Except for this group, other women stayed away and were not seen as part of society. They were called *cheri parathaiyar*. Terms like *uruthira kanigaiyar* and *kanigaiyar* have been used extensively in the five great epics and works of minor literature.

The devadasi system was practised in the Sangam era and till the middle of the 19th century The Sangam literature text, *Pattinapaalai* refers to *kondi magalir* (women who were captured as the spoils of war) who undertook the task of cleaning the temples and lighting the lamps. Temples were a site of plunder, a tool to subjugate people and power centres. People perceived them as divine representations and admired them with devotion. Temples forced women into the system as devadasis to please the powerful and the affluent.

Citing Vemanna, an atheistic Telugu poet of the 17th century, N. Subbu Reddiyar, a well-known scholar in Tamil, Telugu and English at the Sri Venkateswara University, Tirupati, describes one such situation: 'Till the end of the 19th century, it was considered a status symbol for a man to have concubines.' This book offers many such insights about Moovalurar, who fought against a socially deplorable practice, and it has an impressive amount of detail.

Jeevasundari's clear and concise account arranges the events of Moovalurar's life rather like the flow of a river, in linear order, so that they stay in the mind of the reader. The book is short and has nine chapters. The chapter on the social background of the devadasis refers to their origin from the Sangam age in a mere six sentences. I have added a few more details to set the context. The appendices have additional useful information, so readers will not need to search for Moovalurar's works. Extracts from these have been included in the appendices and will help readers get a complete picture of her work and life.

After the Sangam era, women like Madhavi and Manimekalai have been portrayed in the epics as strong women who broke free from the fetters of the devadasi practice. Even they were unable to eradicate the practice. Only Moovalurar worked in the field for abolishing the practice and the law to prevent dedication of women as devadasis. I hope the Tamil-speaking world will make use of this valuable book, which has been published by Pulam Pathippagam.

Hearty congratulations and best wishes to Jeevasundari.

K Thirunavukkarasu
(Researcher on the Dravidian movement)
Mylapore, 2014

Introduction

Some time before the United Nations announced 1975 as International Women's Year, a committee was formed in India to understand the status of women. To a large extent, for the first time in the history of independent India, the report submitted by this committee helped understand the lowly status of women in the political, economic and social spheres as well as the violence perpetrated against them. This report (entitled *Towards Equality: The Report of the Committee on the Status of Women in India*) also includes the role played by the government in enabling women to improve the quality of their lives in future, the blueprint for the working of feminists and activists. The report greatly helped in foregrounding the feminist perspective and women focussed studies on the contributions of women in politics and economics as well as to prepare a plan of action for women's movements. It is not an exaggeration to state that the feminist perspective in social science research in the 1980s and the strengthening of the women's movement were due to this report. Following this, feminists in the departments of history in universities undertook research on the contributions of women in India's freedom struggle. Feminist historians such as Geraldine Forbes, Aparna Basu, Bharati Ray, Kumkum Roy, Tanika Sarkar and Uma Chakravarti pointed out the patriarchal views that were present far and wide in the writing of history. They also described in their research, how history needs to be written from the perspective of women.

A pathbreaking book that was published during this time was *Recasting Women,* a collection of essays, edited by Kumkum Sangari and Sudesh Vaid. This collection, not only examined the contributions of women in social reform movements and politics, thus reviewing the scope of women's history, but also re-evaluated the colonial and Indian social reform movements from a feminist perspective. They helped understand how women's roles were redefined by reformists within the framework of nationalism. Further, the book pointed to the need to identify and contest patriarchal notions that pervaded the historical field, the type of records required to write history from the perspective of women and the ways in which women's identity can be retrieved from the blotted pages of colonial and nationalist discourses.

Despite the fact that such breakthroughs in research methodologies were not extensively discussed in academia, they inspired researchers like me to think about alternative histories. In the late 1980s, as a research scholar at Jawaharlal Nehru University, working on a simple research topic, 'The Contribution of Women to the Freedom Struggle in Tamil Nadu', I reached the Tamil Nadu state archives. Only then did I realise that even historical records had been documented from a patriarchal perspective. Given this, where could I search for historical records outside the state archives? Would any such records that I found be given any consideration by historians? I recall how Kamala Vishweswaran and I had more or less ambushed women who were known to be freedom fighters in Chennai by turning up at their homes unannounced. This enabled me to meet a number of women who had taken part in the Self-Respect Movement. In particular, my meetings and discussions with Comrade Sivagami Chidambaranar, Kudanthai Rajammal Vasudevan (who wrote about the importance of contraception for women in 1934 in *Kudi Arasu*) made me realise how the perspectives of women in the Self-Respect Movement were completely different from those in the freedom movement. This changed the course of my research.

At the same time (in the late 1980s), the field of Subaltern Studies was slowly but surely gaining ground. What type of new records are required to bring to light the lives of people glossed over by history and the lives and struggles of people neglected in history? How do we review the existing historical records from the perspectives of the oppressed? Oral historical records helped in creating a new framework for history and to foreground the lives of subaltern people as important historical events.

Up until now, it would not be wrong to say that Indian history was informed by patriarchal and hegemonic perspectives and written with the help of records that supported these. Thus, the history of the Dravidian movement and associated research on it, were presented with a view that the movement was a divisive one and was supported by the British. This hegemonic view ignored and rejected the fact that this movement worked for the rights of women and other oppressed groups. There was thus a refusal to acknowledge the Dravidian movement as a social reform movement. Against this background, many people with feminist thoughts, and I include myself in this, undertook research on the contributions of women in the Dravidian movement. In 1991, I wrote a research article on Ramamirtham Ammaiyar's novel *Dasigalin Mosa Valai* in *Economic and Political Weekly*. I also wrote an article on the 'Role of Women in the Self-Respect Movement and Feminist Thoughts of Periyar'. This was published in the research journal

Social Scientist (1991). Following this, many feminist thinkers have researched and published articles on Periyar's feminist thoughts and the radical social views of women in the Self-Respect Movement. An important contributor to this type of research is Comrade V Geetha. In the intervening 20 years, many revolutionary things have happened in the rewriting of history from a feminist standpoint. I cannot elaborate them here, but without doubt, Comrade B Jeevasundari's present book occupies a prominent place in this tradition. In particular, this book has brilliantly documented women in politics and history from a feminist perspective. She has written this book so well and it is a testimony to her tireless work, her interest in feminist theory and her commitment to make visible the history of the subaltern. Her feminist research methodologies are evident in the way she has collected historical records and used them. The details about Moovalur Ramamirtham Ammaiyar that have been included in this book were not only unknown till now but also help to review Moovalurar's contribution to the movement and her autobiographical novel. Jeevasundari has meticulously and beautifully described the feminist politics of Moovalurar through many new records such as photos collected from her grandson Selvaraj, interviews with him, her great grand-daughter sharing the handwritten manuscript of Moovalurar's *My Life History* (this is an important record), her undated articles, and those published in *Annai* magazine.

Among the details that Jeevasundari has included which were not known earlier are: the selling of Moovalurar when she was a child to a dasi, her parents abandoning her due to poverty, the penury and violence she faced, her extraordinary knowledge of music and proficiency in Sanskrit, her deep knowledge of Hinduism, how all of these helped her to contest the Hindu religion later, and some historical details about her husband,

Suyambu Pillai. Similarly, the book also records details like how and why Moovalurar joined the Congress and her reasons for leaving that were thus far not known. Jeevasundari has sourced this information from Moovalurar's life history and presented it to us. It is important to highlight how Moovalurar's organization of the first Isai Vellala Sangam (original name Nagapasathar Sangam) Conference in Moovalur, her first experience as a public speaker and her work in the Congress party is presented through interesting anecdotes in the book.

Jeevasundari describes Moovalurar's efforts to support the introduction of the Prevention of Dedication Act by Muthulakshmi Reddy. The author also raises an important question about why Muthulakshmi never wrote or even mentioned such an important woman leader anywhere in her autobiography. This question has to be analysed in depth by historians.

This book includes excerpts from the serialised novel *Damayanti* (1945), her essay on Islam ('Islam and the Status of Indians' 1939), and her famous semi-autobiographical novel *Dasigalin Mosa Valai.*

At a time, when Hindutva forces vehemently propagate their version of the Hindu religion, through it the Brahmanical hegemony and false propaganda against Islam, it is a welcome addition that the essay on Islam has been introduced in this book. In this essay, Moovalurar says that Islam is a democratic religion and it is a welcome move that people have embraced Islam in opposition to the Aryan conspiracy. Through these arguments, we can decipher Moovalurar's views on equality of religions, her arguments on women's rights in Islam and her perspective on Islam from a feminist standpoint. I am extremely happy to note that the present work by Jeevasundari foregrounds a feminist revolutionary who practised feminism, self-respect and anti-caste views in her personal and public lives. It also identifies and documents the life of a braveheart who was the catalyst for the abolition of the Devadasi system and who brought together disadvantaged women from the lowest rungs of society. My best wishes to her as she undertakes more such research.

S Anandhi
(Madras Institute of Development)
Chennai, 2015

Translator's Note

Over a long time, thinkers and intellectuals have discussed, debated and disagreed about what a translation, and by extension, a translator, should or should not do. While we are yet to arrive at a concluding remark on translations and translators, I firmly believe that a translation needs to be responsive to the original text in terms of its language and culture. In this sense, a translator is more of an accomplice to the author of the original text.

My tryst with Moovalur Ramamirtham Ammaiyar happened when I undertook a project on the devadasi system as it exists today for the National Commission for Women, New Delhi, along with Dr M Priyamvadha. Any research on the devadasi system is incomplete without knowledge of the work of Dr Muthulakshmi Reddy and Moovalurar. While resources are available in plenty about the former, there was very little on the latter. It is in this context that B Jeevasundari's Tamil work entitled *Moovalur Ramamirtham: Vazhvum Paniyum* assumes importance. Jeevasundari's slim volume was packed with historical information, archival documents and inspiring details about a legendary personality, whom we have missed in the passage of time. It had a formidable context-setting in the form of prefaces and an introduction by Ayya Chinna Kuthoosi,

Thiru Thirunavukkarasu and Dr S Anandhi. My sincere thanks to them.

- Heartfelt thanks to Jeevasundari for entrusting this translation to me.
- Sincere thanks to Tamil Nadu Textbook and Educational Services Corporation for their yeoman service to the cause of translation.
- Affectionate thanks to Mini Krishnan for being a friend and mentor in all my efforts at translation.
- Many thanks to Urvashi and the team at Zubaan for making the task of publication seem easy.
- Special thanks to Ms A Sivaranchini, for her tireless typing of the manuscript.

V Bharathi Harishankar
Coimbatore, 2023

1

Hidden Histories

New history takes shape when there is a renewal of hitherto invisible histories and this monograph is one such attempt. Moovalur Ramamirtham Ammaiyar was born in 1883 and died in 1962. She lived at a time when Indian history faced major upheavals. In particular, it was a time when women spearheaded protests to liberate themselves from the stranglehold of stifling social customs, which stalked them from birth to death.

Women's protests became visible in India from the mid-19th century on when the direct rule of the British was firmly established in India. They intersected with the freedom struggle, the Self-Respect Movement and also reflected the global ideas of social reform. At that time, the lives of women in India were 'living hells'. A quick illustration of one such deplorable condition of women's lives was the practice of Sati in which the wife was immolated on the funeral pyre of her husband. Protests against child marriage, polygamy, lack of access to education, the dedication of young girls as devadasis and the denial of the right to seek divorce to women were heard everywhere. While men often initiated these protests, gradually women came to be directly involved in them across the country.

It was the collective strength of women's voices from the late-19th to mid-20th centuries that silenced patriarchal dominance, at least to a limited extent.

A nation's independence is often ushered in by ordinary people who occupy the lower rungs of society. They lead their lives as slaves, labourers, farmhands, farmers and the like. They are oppressed and disadvantaged individuals and form 50 per cent of these groups. Thus, freedom for the common people necessarily includes women's liberation. A civilization or nation in which women do not perceive their freedom cannot claim to have attained independence. In India, women's voices played a significant role in the movement for independence, the self-respect movement and in the socialist revolution.

The First Woman Militant

By the late 19th century, the degrading practice of dedicating girls as devadasis was widely prevalent in Tamil Nadu. Moovalurar fought for the liberation of young women from this heinous practice which was like a blot on Indian culture. Her struggle against the practice of dedicating women as devadasis began in the 1910s and intensified in the 1920s. She believed strongly that women's liberation means freedom from the cultural shackles which bound them. She condemned ostentatious weddings and the practice of giving dowry. She travelled across Tamil Nadu and gave public speeches in support of self-respect marriages, inter-caste marriages (anti-caste weddings), widow remarriages and she spoke of the need for simple marriage customs. Nearly 85 years ago she boldly and openly criticized the Hindu Sanatana Dharma. Angered by her militancy, an irate gang of Sanatanists chopped off her hair while she was addressing a public gathering.

Moovalurar's untiring efforts, as the first woman propagandist of the Congress movement in 1920s in Tamil Nadu, were praised by Gandhi Adigal. She remained a friend and compatriot of Thanthai Periyar and walked out of the Congress party along with Periyar and ably supported the Self-Respect Movement founded by him. She popularized Periyar's self-respect marriages and casteless marriages across Tamil Nadu. In all, she was the rising star of women's liberation in Tamil Nadu. However, in her public life, spanning 50 years, she never held any public office till she passed away at the age of 80.

Despite these very significant contributions, to what extent are the life and works of Moovalurar remembered by Tamil society? A marriage scheme was introduced in her name by Kalaignar Karunanidhi during the Dravida Munnetra Kazhagam (DMK) rule. But, have her life and struggles ever been documented in textbooks and books on Indian history? Has her name been effectively represented in the history of the Congress, the Dravidian and women's liberation movements? As a general rule, history glosses over the lives of the oppressed. In the same way, the history of Moovalurar has been swept under the carpet. For instance, her contribution to the abolishing of the devadasi system has not been celebrated to the same extent as that of Dr Muthulakshmi Reddy. This is not surprising because even today, history continues to remain in the hands of dominant caste and class groups. Whereas the history of the subalterns, that is, people who are from humble origins and who lead ordinary lives, is often relegated to the margins.

2

Birth
From Tiruvarur to Moovalur

Although Moovalur Ramamirtham Ammaiyar's name has the prefix Moovalur (indicating the name of the town), she was born in a different place, Tiruvarur. Both these towns were part of the erstwhile unified Thanjavur district. Her childhood was full of misery. Brief accounts of her life have been published in *Kalai Mandram,* a magazine, as well as in other Dravidian movement magazines. These documents describe her childhood as follows:

Her parents belonged to the Isai Vellala community but refused to accept the devadasi tradition. Since they didn't want their daughter to be dedicated as a devadasi, they had to face abject poverty. The fact that she was sold for ₹10 and an old sari describes the extent of the poverty faced by them. Unable to take care of his wife and daughter, her father ran away without informing anybody. The helpless mother sold her daughter to a devadasi. She left quietly in the night after putting the child to sleep. (*Kalai Mandram* 10.04.1954). Some of these details have been mentioned by Moovalurar in her article entitled 'Beware Devadasis' on 13.12.1925 (in *Kudi Arasu*, the magazine). The same details have also been reproduced in Moovalurar's preface to her 1936 novel *Dasigalin Mosa Valai* or *Mathi Petra Minor.* She states that she was forced into the devadasi tradition, came out of it and has vowed to eradicate the tradition. A combination of these details and the information provided by Moovalurar's family members was used to reconstruct her childhood for this book. However, the details about her childhood and growing years were in no way complete. Later, more information came to light while consulting Moovalurar's handwritten manuscript of her memoir and some articles which appeared in 1959-1960 in *Annai* magazine published by the DMK Minister, Satyavani Muthu. These archival resources present a clearer picture of her formative years as well as her struggles with society following her marriage and her battle against the devadasi tradition.

The Paravai Nachiyar Lineage

Moovalurar's father, Krishnaswamy, was from Tiruvarur. Her mother, Chinnammal, belonged to Moovalur. They came from families who practised the dedication of girls (At that time, the term Isai Vellala was not in use). As with the women born in the devadasi clan, the men too were in a pitiable situation. If they were fortunate enough to be musically talented, they could eke a living as musicians. Otherwise they were largely dependent on their sisters who had been dedicated to temples. Social custom dictated that married men within the clan could not give up their daughters for dedication. It was only daughters born to devadasis who could be dedicated.

Even if someone came forward to do so, they lost their standing and respect in the community and were made outcastes. Krishnaswamy had two elder sisters, Chayavathy and Thanga Paapu, and a younger brother, Soundararajan. This family was popularly called the paravai nachiyar (a prominent devadasi clan) lineage. The other siblings in the family were proficient in education and music. 'Even though my father lacked formal knowledge, he had an innate perception. Others would consult my father before starting any work.' Moovalurar mentions this in the handwritten manuscript of her memoir.

Father Runs Away: Krishnaswamy and Chinnammal had only one daughter. Both Chayavathy and Thanga Paapu had been dedicated as devadasis. Since the sisters had no children, they wanted to adopt their niece. However, it was considered lowly to engage the daughter on the paternal side in this profession, and so Krishnaswamy refused to give his daughter for adoption. His sisters were furious and they threw him out of the house. Krishnaswamy's family was on the streets and didn't have the wherewithal to survive.

What kind of job could a man from a devadasi family get? With no means of survival, the family reached Chinnammal's natal home in Moovalur. At the time, Moovalurar was only 4 years old. Her maternal grandmother was also very poor and she could not afford to feed three more people. Despite this, she managed to help them for a year. When the family was in dire straits, Krishnaswamy ran away from home in the night. For men, the easiest way out of tricky situations is to abandon the family. When Chinnammal woke up the next day, she was shocked to find him gone. Even after searching for many days, she was unable to find him. This incident affected Chinnammal's mother: 'This is what happens to a woman married into a devadasi family,' she said. The grief of seeing her daughter and granddaughter in this condition drove Chinnammal's mother to her death. Moovalurar describes her grandmother's death thus: 'Chinnammal's situation became precarious. No one supported them. They were turned away mercilessly everywhere. Six months passed.'

Mother also Escaped: During this time, Moovalurar's father wrote a letter informing his wife about his whereabouts in Chennai.

> I didn't inform anyone when I left. If I had done so, you wouldn't have let me go. I came to Chennai looking for a job but haven't found one. I am doing a menial job in an affluent family. There is no salary but they provide me with food. I don't know how we can manage if you come here. Inform me about your situation.

Chinnammal replied, 'My situation here is worse than yours. My mother is no more. Where can I go? I will come to your place.' Moovalurar was not aware of this correspondence between her parents. However, her mother was restless and her mind was in a turmoil. She thought: 'It's deplorable to dedicate girls born to the men in devadasi families. They will be ostracised. My daughter should not face the problems that I have faced. I should leave her with someone engaged in the devadasi tradition.'

She sold her precious daughter, who she had brought up with so much love, to a devadasi named Aachikannu in Moovalur for ₹10 and an old sari. She left in the night when Moovalurar was asleep and went in search of her husband in Chennai. Moovalurar was 5 years old at the time. She describes this incident in detail in *Kalai Mandram* (issue dated 10.04.1954) as follows: 'Let me give my child to somebody. I have faced misery. At least let her be....'

> Her decision made, she went to Moovalur where a devadasi offered to rear the child. She gave her beloved

child to the devadasi. In the process, she killed the desire to educate her daughter, demolished her dreams of getting her daughter married, curbed her maternal instincts and sold the child.

Yes, the mother abandoned her child. How? What if the child had seen her leaving and asked, 'Amma, where are you going?' Would she not have been overcome with sorrow? She would not have been able to answer the child's simple question. If she wept, the child would have asked, 'Amma, why are you crying?' This would be akin to being pierced by a hundred thousand spears. Having thought through the entire scenario, she put her child to sleep, gave her a last kiss and ran away from penury to a faraway corner of the world.

Moovalurar's life has been combined with a little bit of imagination and presented in this manner.

Training in Music: When she woke up in the morning and found her mother gone, Moovalurar started crying. She describes this in an article in *Annai* magazine.

> I woke up the next morning and couldn't find my mother. When I asked, people said that my mother had gone to Tiruvarur in search of my father. I kept crying and refused to eat anything. That devadasi mother pacified me. She got some new dresses for me and adorned me with some gold trinkets. Since I had never seen them before, I was overjoyed. That lady hired a tutor to teach me. He was a kind person and taught me Tamil, Telugu and Sanskrit. With his affection and my love for learning, I completely overcame the disappearance of my parents. In three years, I became fluent and proficient in the three languages. Then the lady taught me music. In those days, girls who didn't

> know music could not be dedicated as devadasis. It was socially unacceptable. The lady who brought me up hired a teacher to teach me music.

Dandiam Ritual: Three years passed. When Moovalurar turned seven, according to the devadasi customs the anklet or gajja puja was organized as a precursor to the act of dedication. This tradition—which was also propagated by religious custom and ritual—was a way of introducing the young girl meant for dedication to important and eminent people so that they could get acquainted with her. The event was arranged with much pomp and ceremony. Usually, an auspicious day and time would be chosen for the puja and invitations would be sent to important people. Six measures of rice would be spread on the floor. The dance gurus would chant mantras like priests did in temples. The girl about to be engaged as a devadasi would be decorated, made to stand on the rice grains and an anklet tied on her ankle. The two dance gurus, *nattuvanars*, would then hold the pestle which would be decorated with a dhoti at the centre of the rice grains. The girl would also hold the pestle. Then the dance guru would hold the woman's anklet adorned feet and tap on the floor to the rhythm of 'tai…tai'. Then he would announce that the girl who is wearing the anklets and holding the pestle has become a handmaiden of God. The important guests would nod their assent. This was the gajja puja ritual. A girl who undergoes the ritual would be made to wear the bead chain when she attains puberty and is dedicated as a devadasi. Nobody was allowed to marry her. Moovalurar also underwent the gajja puja. She describes it in great detail in her novel *Dasigalin Mosa Valai* or *Mathi Petra Minor*.

Parents in Chennai: What happened to Chinnammal when she went to Chennai in search of her husband? Moovalurar describes her mother's journey as follows:

> Since my mother had already written to my father, he met her at the railway station and took her to the house of Keeranur Govindasamy, a Nagaswaram player. When he saw I was not there, he asked her about me. She said she had left me with Aachikannu akka and that once they were able to earn enough to survive, they could bring me over. My father never raised a question about the logic of leaving a 5-year-old girl behind because he was in abject poverty. My mother earned five rupees as a cook in the house she stayed and she worked as a servant maid in two other houses for six rupees. With a total income of ₹11, they found a room to rent for one rupee in Mandiyar mandapam. Looking at my father's sincerity and capability, the landlady recommended him for a job in a grocery store with a monthly salary of ₹15. My father's skills increased the overall profit of the shop and his salary was increased to ₹20. Put together, the family income rose to ₹40 and my parents stabilized. Even then, they didn't think of bringing me back. The reason was that it became known that I had been sold to a devadasi and they feared that if they took me in, they would have to face criticism and ridicule from society. So they rejected me. Facing acute poverty, they sold me at the age of five. But even when their situation improved, they feared social censure. This fear led them to abandon me. I grew up without experiencing the affection of my parents because of evil social customs.' ('My Life' *Annai* magazine).

After the gajja puja, Moovalurar was introduced to formal music and dance under the tutelage of a well-known nattuvanar (a choreographer and a teacher of dance) called Peralam

Suyambu Pillai. By the age of 10, Moovalurar excelled in dance and music and became popular among music lovers and the earnings she brought in increased. Moovalurar commanded respect in Aachikannu's household. Even though she was very young, she was deeply involved in research work. In general, she was not talkative but would have open-minded discussions with her teachers. In particular, her proficiency in Sanskrit helped her master the details of Puranaic and Vedic rituals. Her discussions with her teachers helped her understand superstitions in the Hindu religion. These intellectual exercises helped her put forward the self-respect ideals later in life.

Fight for Rights for Devadasis

Moovalurar attained puberty at the age of 13. She was a well-known musician and danseuse. After four years, when she turned 17, Aachikannu decided to dedicate her to the temple through the 'Pottu Kattal' ceremony, the ritual through which a devadasi girl is dedicated; officiating for God, the temple priest ties the mangalasutra. She submitted a request to the panchayat board in the temple. As per norms, the temple staff informed the existing devadasis at the temple. They fiercely opposed this proposal because, according to them, although Moovalurar had been brought up by a devadasi, she was from another town and was the daughter of the male heir. They threatened to go to court if this social custom was violated. Aachikannu's dreams were thwarted but Moovalurar was ecstatic. Aachikannu, however, was not willing to let this go. After all, she had to look for a way of getting some income. She tried several ways of getting round this obstacle. At that time, a local merchant, a 'young' man of about 65 claimed he was in love with Moovalurar and came forward to marry her. Aachikannu was overjoyed. Moovalurar describes it thus: 'During that time, a wealthy man came. He was about 65 years old. Beauty and he did not co-exist! He claimed he was in love and wanted to marry me. My foster mother insisted that I married him. I refused. From then on, she started hating me. I also felt that I should leave her but was also worried that there was no one to support me.'

Contract for Life: Moovalurar then decided to marry her music teacher, Suyambu Pillai, who was a patriot and deeply involved in the freedom struggle. He was also someone who disliked blind superstitions and social beliefs. This was the reason she thought he would be a good companion for her. She expressed her feelings to him. 'Aachikannu Amma hates me and I want to leave her. Had I known the whereabouts of my friends, I would have gone to them. But I don't know where they are. You need to help me. It's good that I was not dedicated. Please marry me.'

'Even though you were not dedicated, you went through the gajja puja (preliminaries) and were also a music performer. How can I marry you? If I do, society will ostracize us.'

Despite this concern, however, Suyambu Pillai came forward to marry her. They went to Vazhuvoor temple,* lit a ghee lamp, promised never to part, and put out the light. This was their marriage. The only witness to this marriage was the custodian of Moovalur Margasahaya Swamy temple, Velu Padayachi. The marriage did not follow any religious rituals. Though it was not accepted by the custodians of caste and community, it was a successful marriage. It prospered like the expansive banyan tree. It also served as a union that broke the sentimental beliefs and

---

* Vazhuvoor is a small village near Mayiladuthurai. The temple referred to here is a Shiva temple, whose deity is called Suyambulingaswamy. Moovalurar's husband has been named after this God.

rituals surrounding marriage. It is not an exaggeration to state that it was a forerunner of the self-respect marriage even though it took place before the Self-Respect Movement took shape.

Charge of Murder: Shortly after the marriage, Aachikannu died of cholera. Even though she hated Moovalurar when she was alive, she left all her property to her foster daughter. The sanatana followers who had expected the couple to be made outcastes and wallow in suffering, were annoyed that no such thing happened. So, they started subjecting them to abuse them in different ways. But the Ramamirtham-Suyambu Pillai couple paid no heed and did not worry. After their financial position stabilized, Ramamirtham brought back her parents from Chennai. At that time, she was 25 years old. The conservative forces of society were unable to digest this fact. In particular, the devadasi community did not accept the marriage. They didn't like the fact that a woman brought up for dedication, grew up and did not take up the lucrative job of a devadasi, nor did they approve that she chose her partner herself. So, they conspired in many ways to ruin her life. They were determined to separate the couple and foisted false cases on them. One such was the allegation that Moovalurar had killed another woman. She was not perturbed when the case was filed. She presented the woman she was accused of killing to the court. The woman, who was considered to be dead, explained to the court the torture she had been subjected to and how she was kept in forced confinement. Moovalurar emerged victorious in this murder case. However, social neglect and degradation continued to hound her.

Emergence of a Social Activist: Suyambu Pillai's unstinting support provided the backbone to Moovalurar's surviving social neglect and conspiracies and her emergence as a social activist.

Suyambu Pillai was a Congress supporter and atheist. However, unlike his wife, he never entered active politics. Even so, he was of the view that freedom for women is more important than the country's independence. The first Abolition of Devadasi System conference took place in Moovalur under his leadership. He had spoken and written in support of the Bill to end the devadasi system on various occasions. Suyambu Pillai's moral support was important in enabling Moovalurar to dedicate her entire life as a social activist. His thoughts and views were very much in alignment with hers. The reason is that they traversed the same path.

Moovalur Ammaiyar always wrote her name as Moovalur Ramamirtham. She had not mentioned anything about her birthplace Tiruvarur. The initial 'A' refers to Aachikannu, her foster mother.. With deep gratitude and acknowledgement of Aachikannu's role in bringing her up, Moovalurar put her name as an initial. We can also view this as a remnant of a matrilineal heritage. Many eminent devadasi artists continued this practice. Moovalurar created history by doing this a century ago.

3

Social Background of Devadasis

Moovalurar spent her entire youth protesting against the devadasi system and demanding that it be abolished. Therefore, it is important to understand the plight of women in the social strata she belonged to at least briefly before we discuss her protests and political struggles. Social historians are of the view that the practice of keeping concubines, public women and prostitutes, which has been prevalent since the Sangam age, was later changed to the devadasi tradition, which was deep rooted in several parts of South India. The women in this system were called 'devar adiyar' or handmaidens of god. In Tamil Nadu, the devadasi system was an established practice in the fertile delta districts of Thanjavur, Nellai and Madurai as well as in the Pudukottai kingdom. It was during the Chola reign that women of a particular caste were dedicated as a result of a royal proclamation, thus preventing them from living a marital life.

In 1011 CE/AD, during Rajaraja Chola's reign, lands and houses were given to the dancers in the Thanjai Prahadeeswara temple (Thanjavur). Some of them were even appointed as trustees and managers of the temple. Later, when the temples in the Chola kingdom changed hands and went to the brahmins, these women were slowly eased out of their positions and eventually sent away. This situation of the brahmins taking over the management of temples from the devadasis continued till the modern era and even till contemporary times.

In the devadasi tradition, the act of dedication consisted of several stages with many rituals. Firstly, only the girls belonging to Isai Vellala caste were dedicated as devadasis. The rituals of dedication were similar to those of Brahmin weddings. A young devadasi girl was married to the god even before she attained puberty. The rituals for this marriage were officiated by the priest. During the ceremony, the priest would tie the thali (wedding chain) around the neck of the devadasi girl. This was commonly called 'pottu kattudal'. This was similar to the then prevalent child marriage in the brahmin community.

Nitya Sumangali: In the next step, when the girl attained puberty, a ceremony called 'sadangu' was performed in an ostentatious manner. The expenses for this were borne by the royal family, local landowners, temple trustees and government officers. After this, the sacred ritual of dedicating that young woman as a handmaiden to one temple was conducted. In this important ritual, it was announced in public that she was the handmaiden of god, 'devar adiyar'. These women later came to be known as devadasis. However, because of this ritual, the devadasi was considered to be 'nitya sumangali', one who is not touched by widowhood and who is free from bonds. That is, she was in principle free to have sexual relationships with a person of her choice. Suffice it to say that these sexual partners were mostly landowners and temple trustees. The same people also controlled and managed the revenue of the temple and were mostly brahmins or other upper caste Hindus. If this was so, how was a devadasi free to choose her partner? Why was it announced that way? Isn't there a contradiction here?

Economic benefits: The benefactors and sexual partners of the devadasi gifted lands to them, the control and land documents of these gifts were vested with the temple. No rights over property were given in the name of the devadasi. They were only entitled to the income generated from the property, and this they could enjoy across generations. However, the unwritten norm was that the devadasi had to make sure that she left a female child to continue the tradition. This was considered to be her duty. This genealogy was ensured through dedication of 'minor' (underage) girls. Usually, girls below the age of 12 underwent the ritual of 'pottu kattudal.'

The children of devadasis were prevented from engaging in other professions. Only by making her daughter a devadasi, could a woman get her salary from the temple. A devadasi who did not dedicate her daughter to the temple did not have a peaceful old age. In the same way, any girl who was not dedicated as a devadasi could not enjoy or have access to the property. A devadasi, who did not have a daughter, was permitted to adopt a girl according to Hindu religious customs. It is noteworthy that other Hindu women had no right to adopt or indeed any right to the property. In the Hindu religion, such rights were not granted to women. Men took the decisions. But, in the Devadasi community, women were granted the right to adopt. This was but a 'mere token' of the hegemonic powers to keep a community subservient.

A devadasi entertained her patron in the evening through music and dance and provided sexual comfort in the night. The sexual relationship between a devadasi and her patron did not give her the status or rights of a wife, and she could not interfere in matters of the patron's household.

Men in the Devadasi Community: Men in the devadasi community were variously known as melakarars, nayanakarars and nattuvanars, nagaswaram players, thavil players and dance choreographers. Earlier the community was known as melakara caste. They were sons of devadasis or artists engaged to play musical instruments at temples. There was also a subsect called chinna melam who were accompanying artists during the song and dance performances of devadasis, who played instruments and conducted (nattuvangam) the dance. Sexual relationships between devadasi women and the chinna melam group were banned.

There was also a subsect known as periya melam or nayanakarars. They performed at palaces and during community festivals, when the devadasis did not perform. Their fortunes depended on the patronage received from landlords. Because of this there were little or no sexual relationships between the periya melam and the devadasis. In brief, the idea that devadasis could independently choose their sexual partners, as the conservatives maintained, was a mere verbal gimmick. That they lived under the complete control of the landowners was the ground reality.

The men of the devadasi community who were not proficient in music or education invariably depended on their devadasi sisters for their sustenance. Colloquially, they were called 'mama.' Not all girls born to a devadasi were dedicated. Some could marry, and men of the devadasi community could marry them. However, girls born in the male lineage could not be dedicated and the community did not support it. These women were protectively kept away from the public eye.

Ritual Privileges of a Devadasi: The relationship between landlords and devadasis was not merely sexual. Devadasis had to perform and assist in auspicious occasions in the households of affluent families and landowners. They were also invited to the weddings in their families, and it was seen as a matter of pride and a status symbol to invite devadasis. On behalf of the groom, it was the devadasi who tied the thali around the bride's neck. Just as the temple administration accorded to them the status of nitya sumangali—one who will not be a widow—they were also given the importance to perform these rituals.

Similarly, when a devadasi died, her last rites were performed on behalf of the temple, and the temple was closed for the day. As a mark of mourning and ritual impurity, no pujas were conducted in the temple. The sandalwood, rose water and flowers to be placed on the dead were sent by the temple. Before the final procession and its rituals, the corpse was laid near the front entrance of the temple. However, this does not mean that the devadasis commanded high respect. Both the groups who supported or opposed the devadasi system looked down upon them.

Social Pressures on Devadasis: There were many social restrictions on devadasi men and women on enjoying the monetary benefits received from the temple. Theirs was a double oppression: it was not enough to be a ritual slave of the temple. It was expected that a devadasi would also follow community norms. The handmaidens of god were forced to be sexual paramours of the socially powerful across generations. If they opted out of the devadasi system or were unable to produce a female heir, they lost their privileges and were summarily thrown out of community. This devadasi set up was framed keeping in mind the pleasure of the landowners. That is why the handmaidens of god were derogatorily called 'thevadiya' or cheap prostitutes.

The handmaidens of god recruited during the Chola period were thoroughly degraded as the domination of brahmins grew. During the later reigns of Pandyas, Nayaks and Marathas, they came to be considered as prostitutes. In later years, there were many attempts to procure not only devadasi women but also others from disadvantaged groups and bring them under this practice. Many stone inscriptions and manuscripts have been found as evidence of this.

As mentioned earlier, the devadasi system flourished in Thanjavur, Tirunelveli, Madurai and Pudukkottai districts and Thanjavur topped the list. The Isai Vellala community, who were the custodians of traditional music and dance, were unable to break the shackles that bound them. Across Thanjavur, hundreds of temples had enslaved thousands of Isai Vellala families. The sanatins, landowners, and mutt heads (protectively) ensured that the ritual slavery was kept alive.

Birth of the Polestar: Moovalurar was one such polestar born in a devadasi family at Tiruvarur in the unified Thanjavur district. She was born into a poor family, who had stepped away from the devadasi system. Even so, she was forced into the devadasi practice and faced degradation and shame. That was when she vowed to banish this deplorable practice from the country.

Her family provides a good example of the plight of a family belonging to the Isai Vellala caste which refuses to follow the devadasi tradition. In the note written by Moovalurar, she claims that her parents in fact pushed her into the devadasi system. New documents (after the publication of the first edition of Jeevasundari's book) also confirm this information. Those details have been recorded in the previous chapter. Moovalurar's childhood reveals how extreme poverty faced by a family which resisted the devadasi tradition in fact forced them to accept the same deplorable practice towards the end of the 19th century.

The Oath of the Morning Star: As a way of creating awareness about the devadasi system, Ammaiyar sorrowfully records her rage and resentment about the lives of the devadasis in the Preface to her novel *Dasigalin Mosa Valai* or *Mathi Petra Minor.*

> Devadasi–handmaiden of god. Aha! What lovely descriptors! A devadasi is one who serves god with utmost devotion. When we hear these names now, what thoughts do we have? A home-breaking prostitute is the image we get and not even in our dreams do we think of a devoted spiritual individual. The pundits quoting religious scriptures state that devadasis lived in temples, and were not involved in profane worldly activities and are devoid of worlldly pleasures and dedicated to the service of god. Let alone the present, has there been any time in the past when devadasis lived on earth adhering to the aforementioned description? Only the pundits have to provide the answers. My ordinary brain cannot comprehend this truth even at a miniscule level. In the present time, we don't need to refer to the sastras to understand the devadasis. I think the single description 'thevadiyal magane' captures the lofty sacred ideals of the system.
>
> Devadasi, thevadiyal, kalaipendu, vilai magal and parathai are names used to refer to prostitutes. There are people who distinguish between devadasis and cheap prostitutes. But no one can deny that from ancient times, generations of women have been forced into ritual slavery in the name of god, art and wealth by temple priests, kings, aristocrats and others. Therefore it is futile to argue the inequalities or to glorify them.

Moovalurar had firsthand experience of this deplorable practice when she was forced into dedication as a devadasi. She studied in detail the Hindu texts that supported the devadasi system. She took an oath and considered it as her life's mission to abolish the system. She completely broke free from it.

4

Self-Respect based Political Career of Women

Moovalurar and Suyambu Pillai had a love marriage. They met at the temple and took a vow never to part and started living together. The community did not accept this and people of their own caste condemned them. But they lived without paying any heed to this. Their musical expertise helped them earn a livelihood and soon her parents joined them. Moovalurar refused to settle into this comfortable existence. She brought together a group of people who were unaware of their degraded situation and organized massive protests. These provided a beginning to her political career. At first, she started the Nagapasattar Sangam. She explains it as follows:

> My parents joined me when they came to know that I was leading a respectable life. Taking care of the family became easy. I was 25. Like one possessed, I started making derogatory speeches against the devadasi practice. I faced a lot of problems. I was implicated in a case of murder; there was also a case filed accusing me of luring—with money and jewellery—and kidnapping devadasis. Caste based

restrictions; all these intrusions happened. My husband was afraid. I calmed him down, 'Don't be afraid! If we cannot earn a living, we'll perform on the streets and beg. If people question us, we will explain the deplorable situation. We'll make the public aware of this so they think ill of these people.' Since we were well-versed in music and dance, we taught them to a lot of people and earned a good amount. Since we were thrifty in running the household, we saved a lot and bought land, a house and jewellery and became respectably rich. Others started talking about the rise in my fortune. I made them realize the distinction between a respectable and a deplorable existence. (*My Life History*: handwritten manuscript).

Acquaintance with Gandhi: During this time, Moovalurar was not aware of political parties—in particular, the Congress party—their functions or about the freedom movement. How, then, did she join the Congress?

I had no knowledge about any political party. I learnt Tamil from Moovalur Singaravel Pandit. I had stopped my music profession. At this time, Gandhiji spoke in the north about the 'Fallen Sisters.' It was reported in the newspapers and the Pandit gave it to me. I read it and cried.

'Why do you cry?' he asked.

'You have taught me about our land as the place inhabited by virtuous women and courageous mothers. Can women be engaged in prostitution in god's name? Tamilians are not ashamed of it but I thought about how a man from the north—Gandhi—was aware of these noble women. I cried.' From then on, I started selling khadi clothes. I didn't become a member. I was 35 years old. (*My Life History*: handwritten manuscript).

One of the reasons why Moovalurar joined the Congress movement was because of the support given by some Congressmen to the devadasi cause. When Gandhiji visited and learnt about the prevalence of devadasi system, he was shocked. He also interacted with some devadasis and learnt about their plight, and he referred to them as 'fallen sisters.' Gandhi exhorted Congress leaders to create awareness and work for the total abolition of the devadasi tradition in India, wherever it was prevalent. And it was thus that this issue caught people's attention across the country. Gandhi also wrote a letter of appreciation to Moovalurar after hearing about her passionate protests against the devadasi system.

In those times, it was rare for women to participate directly in social reform movements. We can surmise that what attracted Gandhi to Moovalurar was the fact that a victim of a discriminated community had come forward to fight the evil. 35 years later when a trophy was presented to Moovalurar by the Dravida Munnetra Kazhagam (DMK) party, Annadurai appreciated her work and remarked, 'When the late Gandhiji was in search of women who would work for the social cause 35 years ago, he could find only Ammaiyar.'

She raised a clarion call against the devadasi system, her voice rang aloud far and wide.

Ammaiyar and Khadi: One of the main weapons of the Civil Disobedience Movement was the wearing of khadi. The British obsession on depleting Indian resources was restrained somewhat by the making and wearing of khadi clothes. Since everyone—educated, literate, illiterate—started wearing khadi, the attraction towards foreign cloth waned. The then Congress leader EV Ramasamy (EVR or EVR Periyar) toured the length and breadth of Tamil Nadu in support of the khadi.

He campaigned in support of khadi. As a result of his efforts, khadi selling outlets came up across the state. Indeed, it was EVR who opened the Khadi Spinning Ashram in Tiruchengode which was created by C Rajagopalachari.

After joining the Congress, the charkha and khadi became an integral part of Moovalurar's life. She strictly adhered to the Gandhi-Periyar path both in social reform ideals and the khadi movement. She carried bales of khadi and stitched clothes from town to town and street to street and sold them. Needless to say, she only wore khadi. She also persuaded devadasis, who broke free from the practice, to wear khadi. It seems she would sit at the roadside, sing songs even while spinning the charkha. A crowd would gather on the spot and she would campaign for khadi and charkha. Due to her efforts, many women of the devadasi community became engaged in weaving khadi.

Khadi, the symbol of the Swadeshi movement, became a tool of social reform in the hands of widows, destitute and 'fallen' women in Tamil Nadu. Ashrams, homes for destitute women and centres which worked for banning prostitution were formed and started weaving khadi clothes. Congress leaders carried bales of khadi cloth on their heads and went from home to home and thus formed a large swadeshi network. Moovalurar served as an important link in this network. In this manner, she was passionately involved in the propaganda of the Congress party for three years without any formal knowledge of politics or the freedom movement. She was a living example and her involvement bears testimony to the impact of the Congress movement among common people. It is another matter that later the same Congress party lost its hold on people.

No entry for people not wearing Khadi: The massive Congress movement was a strange combination of a few wealthy people and a large section of people who lived in abject poverty. To equalize things, Gandhi called for people who believed in the ideology of the Congress to live in huts. We do not know how many rich Congressmen moved to huts but Moovalurar, who was living in a tile roofed house, shifted to a hut that she constructed near her house. She also put up a notice board at the entrance of the hut made of braided coconut fronds: 'People not wearing khadi are not allowed inside/to enter.'

During this time, some khadi garments kept in her house were stolen. The Assistant Superintendent of Police from Kuthalam came to her house in uniform and was dumbstruck on seeing the notice outside. He hesitated to enter because he was not wearing khadi and then went into the house from the back entrance. During the interrogation, it emerged that a woman had stolen the khadi garments. The judge asked Moovalurar what punishment he should give to the culprit. She said, 'This woman stole because she did not have a sari to replace the one she was wearing. I appreciate the fact that she is wearing khadi and I withdraw the case.'

Involvement in Congress: 'I joined the Congress at the age of 38 because the party was working for social reforms. In particular, I felt I can work for the abolition of the devadasi system. Congress people in this state used to shower me with praises. I achieved as much fame as the insults I had borne from the same community earlier. I was in the midst of respectable people as an honoured guest.' She recalled with pride the recognition given to her by the Congress in the handwritten manuscript of *My Life History*.

During this period, the State Congress Conference that was held in Peralam, Suyambu Pillai's hometown, assumed importance in Moovalurar's life. Congress leader Thiru Vi Ka Mudaliar was expected to be the Chairman. Some important

Congressmen like Karukudi Chinnaiah Pillai and Kumbakonam Pantulu Iyer came in person to invite Moovalurar. 'I asked them what is meant by a conference…they took me along…I heard Thiru Vi Ka's speech for the first time. Since I had never heard a public speech till then, I was exhilarated. I spoke next. Since there were no other women public speakers in Tamil Nadu, they were generous in their praise for me.' Moovalurar refers to this experience in her autobiography. Her status in her community rose because of her entry into politics and the fame she gained.

> Mother, father and husband were very happy. Some intelligent devadasi women also decided to leave the profession on seeing the respect I received. People who supported me included young and proficient musicians like Koorainadu Thillaiammal and Chidambaram Janakathammal. Then they made me a member of the Zilla Committee, State Committee and All India Committee. Since they were young, people would pass comments on them but they never bothered about them. Congress members protected and respected them. I was happy. I wanted to accomplish my mission with the help of these two women.

She was confident and hopeful.

Nagapasathar Sangam: At this time, there was a plan to send two dancers from Thanjavur to England. An agreement was signed after giving an advance. Condemning this act, the doyen of Nagaswaram and Lion of the Self-Respect ideology, Thiruvaduthurai TN Rajaratnam Pillai published a public notice. This rejuvenated Moovalurar. She was proud that she had found a strong pillar of support.

> That notice was 'strongly worded.' I read it and felt like a pauper unearthing a treasure. I went to Rajaratnam Pillai and expressed my views. 'I have joined Congress for this purpose. If you support me, I will work for the cause of this community.' He joyously supported me. I found two women and a renowned vidwan in my 25-30 years of working for social cause.

Two more women travelled from place to place selling khadi and also campaigned against the devadasi system. Thillaiammal and Janakathammal accompanied Moovalurar everywhere. She spoke of them, 'We made public speeches. I understood that men cannot ruin their lives if women were firm and steadfast.'

The Congress leadership was awestruck by the tireless efforts of these women. Moovalurar's political entry happened at a time when it was a rare sight to find a woman campaigner. Therefore, Congress leaders like Thiru Vi Ka, Varadarajulu Naidu, S Ramanathan, EV Ramasamy Periyar, N Dhandapani projected Moovalurar as the jewel in the crown. They willingly came forward to support her cause. Thiru Vi Ka and EV Ramasamy emphasized the need to form a structured team for Moovalurar's campaign.

> At that time, comrades like Thiru Vi Ka, Varadarajulu and E V Ramasamy Periyar felt that 'it would be useful to form a community-based association and work for the cause of the devadasis. We will extend our full support.' They were important members of the Congress. 'I don't know how to run an association,' I said. They enlisted the help of comrade S V Lingam. Since he was an upcoming loyalist with not enough monetary support he stayed in my house for a year. Our first job was to print a form for member subscriptions. Thillaiammal, S V Lingam and I travelled

all over Tamil Nadu, especially Ramanathapuram, Tiruchi, Thanjavur, North Arcot districts and obtained signatures from people who agreed to join the association. We also met people who were hidden from the public and sought their support. Nagapasathar Sangam was formed in this manner. Had it not been for S V Lingam's unstinting support, it wouldn't have been possible. The credit for the upliftment of the community goes to him. He also mentored me about the intricacies of politics.' Moovalurar recalls the formation of Nagapasathar Association in this manner.

S V Lingam, who is described by Ramamirtham Ammaiyar with such gratitude, has also been well-represented by K Thirunavukkarasu in his book *Pillars of Dravidian Movement* (p.47) as follows:

> From what we have read and heard about him, that he was a unique personality was readily apparent. In brief, if we need to identify him, he was similar to the character Mannangkatti in the silent play *Peace* written by the revolutionary poet Bharathidasan or the 'White dhoti clad Samiyar' in the short novel of Arignar Anna called *Last Burglary*. SV Lingam appears to be a combination of these two characters.

Thirunavukkarasu also refers to Karaikudi Rama Subbaih's description of S V Lingam in his book.

> S V Lingam used to talk humorously. He would not hide his emotions and brood over things. He was open and blunt in expressing his views; he was short, he played a major role in the progress of the party! He was a true socialist. He would leave town only with the dhoti and shirt he wore.

> Wherever he went and with whichever friend he stayed, he would borrow a dhoti and shirt, wash the ones he wore and moved to the next town. He wouldn't return what he received and he felt that things should have a timely use for the people who need. His idea was that things should not be hoarded citing ownership.

First Isai Vellala Conference: Later, S V Lingam decided to rename the Nagapasathar Sangam.

> Since this practice was followed citing different caste names, we wanted one unifying name. We met many pundits and my master Moovalur Singaravel suggested 'Isai Vellala' as the nomenclature. He cited evidence from the text *Santha Divakaram*. Vellalar's undertake different occupations—farming, cow herding, grocery, what the world considers morally depraved occupations. All jobs are that of the same caste. I also wondered why the musical profession should belong to the lower caste? (*My Life History*: handwritten manuscript).

Moovalurar describes why a respectable name was required to refer to a socially deplored community. The first Isai Vellala conference was held in Moovalur and she financed it out of her own funds.

> I conducted it under the Chairmanship of Comrade Singaravel. The Chairman of the reception committee was my husband Suyambu. Many dignitaries attended the conference. The discourse by Thanjavur K. Natarajan was emotionally stirring. Some men who depend on these women for their sustenance and some women who practised the devadasi system opposed it.

Against Devadasi Practice: In her article entitled 'Beware Devadasis' which appeared in *Kudi Arasu* in 1925, Moovalurar describes her early protests against the devadasi system.

> I have strived to stop and abolish the devadasi practice for seven or eight years. Last year, I conducted a conference in order to bring about a social reformation and to make them virtuous women. Even without invitations, I have attended weddings and spoken to people about the dedication of women and obtained promises from many women not to indulge in or force their sisters into prostitution. This year also I had invited national leaders to speak about this practice in the second conference. Some opportunists claimed during the marriage last week in Vila Nagar that I am infusing new ideas in men and women. They have described me as an axe which mangles tradition. They have threatened to manhandle me and make me an outcaste if I speak on the occasion of any marriage.... How can such depraved men who lead their lives at the expense of women be called men?

It was quite natural that Moovalurar held strong views against the devadasi system, having been raised within a devadasi family. This period witnessed many reformist initiatives in India. To begin with, her protests were not aligned to a movement. They were practical and on-the-ground activities. She would visit houses and talk privately to young girls who had been dedicated, she would recount her experience and advise them to come out of the system. She would secretly help the women who did so to leave their homes and find means of livelihood. She bore whatever troubles came her way with fortitude. She also helped many devadasi women who managed to break away from the system to get married and she formed the organization, Nagapasathar Sangam, with these women.

> How many marriages have I conducted? How many public orations? How many times have I gone from door to door? How many private conversations? They cannot be counted. I faced a lot of cases because I got the devadasi women to break free and get married. I did not stop my work out of fear. Nor was I affected by the cases. I got free advertisement and became famous. (*My Life History*: handwritten manuscript). She successfully conducted two conferences through this association.

Protest by the Devadasi Community: There was a strong backlash from the devadasi community against the abolition of the devadasi system.

> At a time when I was deeply concerned about ways to put an end to this group of prostitutes, who had broken away from the system, this opportunity was a godsend. I formed the Pottuaruppu Sangam or anti-dedication associations and started campaigning extensively. The opposition from the community, the powerful leaders, Brahmin priests, zamindars, landlords and pimps was overt and covert. My friends and I felt overwhelmed. We came to the conclusion that it was easier to fight against the British and Brahmin hegemony than fight for the abolition of the devadasi system...' (Preface to *Mathi Petra Minor*).

Even so, she confronted the opposition and won. Despite opposition from the devadasi community, gradually devadasi women joined the Pottuaruppu Sangam. Self-respected musicians such as Thiruvavaduthurai T N Rajaratinam Pillai and Seerkazhi P N Subbiah Pillai gave unstinting support to her. She fought against the devadasi system because it was deplorable but she had a lot of affection towards devadasi women and the community. This is why she never retaliated against their attacks and their attempts to thwart her efforts. However, the attacks against her were not only brutal but also lethal. That violence against a woman targets her femininity and to humiliate her is proven by some incidents in her life.

Artistic Career: There are some references to Moovalurar acting in some plays. We can safely assume that the plays were political ones that questioned the devadasi system. Further, Arumugham Chettiar, a 77-year old man living in Moovalur, said that in her old age, she taught music to schoolgirls. In an interview, he said:

> In the chariot lane near Lord Margasahaya temple, there was a pyol school. When I was four, I was admitted into that school. Girls and boys were seated on opposite pyols. Moovalur Ammaiyar's house was right across this school. That is, from the main road leading to Mayavaram, her house was on the left and the Theradi lane was on the right. On days when she wasn't addressing public meetings or conferences, she would cross the road and come to Theradi lane. In the pyol school, she would teach music and lessons on different subject to girls. After some time, she would go about her business.

Moovalurar's contemporary and the sculptor of the idols in Mayiladuthurai Mayuranatha Swamy temple, Kandasamy Thevar, used to act in plays with her. Even though he passed away, his grandson and retired teacher, Sitharkadu Meenakshi Sundaram, said about the violence meted out to her is shocking. According to him, the sanatana followers could not digest her opposition to the devadasi system and the fact that she performed plays about this. They sent her several warnings. When they fell on deaf ears, they were furious.

They came in a group and climbed up onto the stage. She was in the middle of a performance, they chopped off her hair with an axe but she did not stop her performance. Moovalurar refused to be cowed down by this brutal act. She continued her propaganda more fiercely. The incident sent shock waves in that region. Meenakshisundaram, a teacher who is known to the author, recalled how his father could never come to terms with the incident and kept referring to his sense of helplessness. There is no written evidence for this anecdote. However, Moovalurar's family confirmed it, although they were surprised that I had heard of it. According to her family, she refused to let her hair grow after this and kept it cropped till her dying day. There is another story in her life that lends credence to the story of her hair being chopped off.

> In Omampuliyur, I once stayed in the house of an Isai Vellala woman. I was conversing with a few people on the veranda. The lady gave me some milk. I drank it and it burnt into me like fire. I immediately spat it out. Within a few minutes, my face was swollen and my tongue was hanging loose. Friends who tested the milk were shocked to find that it contained a poison called 'veeram'. Despite my friends telling me I should inform the police, I refused to do so. The woman who gave me the milk had decided to eliminate me because I was trying to abolish the devadasi system. I was sorry about her ignorance. (*Art of Sewing* magazine, May 1959 issue).

People may find it surprising that Moovalurar did not want to take action against the woman who tried to kill her or the sanatanis who chopped off her hair in public. But social reformers have always lived this way. In the battle that they fought, they believed that love and compassion were the foundation. They tirelessly fought against social restrictions that came in the way. For this cause, they bore the pain and the shame. They pardoned the offenders and refused to fight against anyone, especially ignorant people. Moovalurar, who trod this difficult path, faced more tribulations because she was a woman.

Staunch Campaigner for Congress: Moovalurar's political life only had a forward march. The Congress ideology and the abolition of the devadasi system consumed her entire life. She looked frail and aged even while she was still young. No Congress meeting was conducted without her presence. She occupied a prime position on the dais during the conferences at Tiruvannamalai, Salem, Kanchipuram and many other places. When Thiru Vi Ka went on a walking campaign tour of the erstwhile unified Thanjavur district (including Thanjavur, Thiruvarur and Nagapattinam) she accompanied him.

Her political service was deeply appreciated by Thiru Vi Ka. He fully supported her protests against the devadasi system and continued to write against it in his *Navashakti* newspaper. In 1925, he took part in the Isai Vellala conference organized by Moovalurar in Mayiladuthurai. He has described the conference and Moovalurar's life in his autobiography. That helps us understand the work undertaken by her in the Congress party.

> A woman's conference was organized in 1919 in the north. Devadasis were not included. Arputhananda Swamigal wrote an article in *Desa Bhaktan* questioning this. An editorial was written and some articles were received from Tirunelveli, where a conference was also conducted. I heard that communal elements ruined it.

Who is a dasi? Who is a devadasi? The meaning is clear. Both terms have good connotations but came to acquire different meanings later. Gandhiji used to refer to them as 'fallen sisters'. I started using the term as well. 'The reason for the fallen status of women was the baser instincts of men.' These thoughts were spoken and written, thus kindling the right spirit, which helped my endeavours. At Kapaleeswaram, dasis used to come with a divine aura wearing the sacred ash. However, even in that state, some men would look at them with a sexual intent.

Why should these women be dedicated and restrained from marrying? The act of not marrying in the regular sense leads to their downfall. It's better that they marry. Courage is required for a man to marry them. The ones who come forward to marry them are the true reformers and patriots.

These thoughts of mine were later published in *Desa Bhaktan*.

Mayavaram Karpagam

'There was a Nagapasathar Sangam in Mayavaram, which was later changed to an Isai Vellala Sangam. Moovalurar was a pillar of support to this sangam. I was acquainted as a reader of Moovalurar's writings in *Navashakti*. She was so passionate that she started spreading the message and considered it her prime service and duty.

Mayavaram became a fortress for the Congress in Thanjavur. This bastion was guarded by a few people and Moovalurar was one of them. In those days, she admired Gandhism and was deeply inspired by it and she became very good at using the charkha. Every time I went to Thanjavur district for Congress work, I saw her hard at work.

Moovalurar was competent and assumed leadership roles effortlessly. Wherever she went, she would be surrounded by the fallen sisters. In that group, complaints would be brought to her and she would resolve them. I thought of her as a Karpagam (the wish-filling tree) for the women. She organized a conference in 1925 in Mayavaram.

It was not an easy task to convene the Isai Vellala conference. I am aware of the difficulties involved. Moovalurar's efforts made it simple and easy. Congress leaders Mayuramani Chinnaiah Pillai and S Ramanathan supported her. Initially, they wanted me to lead the conference. "It is only appropriate that a Isai Vellala person occupies the Chair. I will provide constant support and be present throughout; I will provide support through *Nava Shakti* as well," I promised. An Andhra lady, Yamuna Purna Tilakamma, who had started a school for fallen sisters called "Yuvathi Saranalayam" was chosen as the chairperson of the conference. I met her and Dhandapani Pillai at Egmore. All of us went to Mayavaram. Ramsamy Naicker also accompanied us. The conference venue became an idyllic garden and all the sisters were like beautiful statues. I shouldn't keep describing the scene. My speech went on for 2½ hours but it felt like 2½ minutes. After this, Ramasamy Naicker took the stage.

My friend is a scholar but inexperienced. I am experienced. He spoke crudely and bluntly. The leaders looked crestfallen and so did the others. The joyous atmosphere faded. There were some exchange of letters between the chair and some of the sisters. 'I think you didn't like my speech,' Naicker said and continued his Khadi campaign. Dhandapani Pillai who spoke after him took on a proselytizing tone and kept providing illustrations for Naicker's statements. His speech was humorous.

Reports

Reports were collected that evening. They were not published but are recalled by those who remember. I present three samples.

- A wealthy landlord had an Isai Vellala concubine. She conceived. The old man wanted her to abort but the attempt failed and the child was born. Immediately, the landlord ordered the mother to cast off the child in the Cauvery river. What did the poor mother do? She lied to him but left the child in a safe place. This is an abstract of one report.
- One sister reformed, thanks to the efforts of the Isai Vellala Sangam. She wanted to become a teacher. On learning about this, the Mirasudar disfigured her face. This is the essence of a report.
- A young, intelligent woman was present. I asked her if she wanted to go to school. She shed tears on hearing this. 'How can I get an education? Can I go out of this place? Impossible. There's constant watch on me, even in this street.' I asked her who will 'behead' her. Another sister sitting beside her mentioned a name and said, 'the head of this mutt.' My pen fell down. This is the gist of another report.

Many wrote reports. If these truths are published, the world will be forced to look for the guillotine. (*Life Notes of Thiru. Vi.Ka.* Kazhagam Publications pp. 599-604).

Dancing Flag: The All India Congress conference took place in Kakinada. The British had passed a sudden order banning any flag march. 'You'll prevent me only if I carry the flag.' The British government was truly amazed when Moovalurar stitched a few flags together and wore then as a sari and joined the procession as a dancing flag. Describing this, she writes:

> When I was in Congress, I received the 144 ban order thrice from the British government. I defied the orders. They banned the carrying of the flag by hand in procession. I combined the tricolours of saffron, green and white into a sari and wore it to the Kakinada Congress conference. People looked joyously at me in the conference. Mohammed Ali Jinnah asked for the details. I responded stating that it's a crime to hold the flag in your hand but what can they do if it's worn as a sari? They gave me a certificate commending me as a 'Braveheart of Tamil Nadu.' I have received many such medals. (*My Life History*: handwritten manuscript).

On another occasion, she was restrained from speaking in public as she stood on a stage. She then placed a blackboard on stage and wrote her entire speech out and created a headache to the police.

Many people joined the freedom movement and the social reform movement after listening to speeches by leaders and reading their works. However, very few joined the movement after analysing their own lives and looking for change in personal life and society. Moovalurar entered the fray with a dream of a new society. That was the reason why her protests were without compromises, were incisive, and without an iota of pretence.

In a society where women were devadasis and prostitutes, she entered politics with the hope of reforming and rejuvenating society. She didn't compromise or negotiate on using the political organ for her social cause. This was readily apparent during her days in the Congress and later in the Self-Respect Movement.

The Dhoti-wearing Campaign: Whatever Gandhi said was like an order for Moovalurar. She would fulfil his wishes as if she were his first, loyal follower. She was the first to respond to Gandhi's plea against untouchability. Bound by the complete domination of the landowners, for centuries, dalits were not allowed to wear dhotis. Moovalurar helped them wear dhotis for the first time. She wrote:

> I read in the magazine about Gandhiji's reforms for the Adi Dravidar Community. Immediately, I left for Moovalur. I called the Adi Dravida men and gave them khadi dhotis, made them wear them and took them in a procession singing patriotic songs. In those days, Adi Dravidas were not supposed to wear the dhoti around the waist. They were supposed to wear only a loincloth and wind the dhoti on their head. This was the practice then. When they put on dhotis around their waists and sang along with me, the Mirasudar men beat them up.
>
> 'You dare wear a dhoti around your waist? Can a pariah sing?' they were furious.
>
> They came and pleaded with me. The next day I took them and met the Mirasudar, 'It seems you beat them yesterday because they had worn a dhoti. Today they have come respectfully in their loincloth. Are you happy?'
>
> Without saying a word, he went in. The Congressmen praised me for accomplishing this task for the first time in Tamil Nadu. I was lauded a thousand times more than I was degraded by my community. The group was decimated. I was surrounded by respectable people.

Gandhi gave a call to engage harijans in households so that the discrimination would end and they would be treated as fellow human beings. Moovalurar employed Ratinam, a Dalit girl in her house. She recalls, 'Gandhiji spoke about employing Harijans. Immediately I employed an Adi Dravida girl, Ratinam, in my house. The caste fanatics made my house untouchable. No one would come there. But Congressmen visited and praised me. Only after this did Karukudi Chinnaiah Pillai and Marudur Kandasamy Pillai come as equals.'

Protest against the oppression of some people had remained till her last breath. She was focussed on creating awareness among dalits. Having grown up among them, she used her clout to campaign for prohibition of alcohol and the importance of education. She would host a veritable feast at her house with vadai and payasam for dalits. However, she put the conditions that to take part in the feast as equals, they should abstain from consuming alcohol and wear a dhoti.

> Because I employed the girl, Ratinam, the Adi Dravida people supported me with affection and listened to me. I would speak in their meetings. If they fell ill or faced other troubles, I would go in person and help them. I made a small thatched hut near my house and taught them to read and write. I bought slates and books at my own expense. I would instruct the women to keep the streets clean and maintain hygiene. If they didn't listen, I would go to the *Cheri* and clean. The next day they would ensure the streets were cleaned before I reached for fear that I would do it. I was a guide and transformed them. Knowing that I would scold them if I found them drinking, they would do it stealthily. Many overcame the habit. Recalling the day Gandhiji was imprisoned, I would host a grand feast once a year. Teetotallers and those wearing dhotis were allowed. I would insist on feeding those wearing only loincloth or consuming alcohol and would make them eat outside the house. Those who mended their ways ate inside the house and had a feast with vadai and payasam. Others ate outside but were banned from eating the delicacies. 'If you mend

> your ways, there are no restrictions,' I would advise them. As years went by, I found more people joining the feast inside the house. These people offered unstinting support wherever I went.

Moovalurar's society-focused political activities fill us with a sense of wonder.

Sanatana Nandhi: Multifaceted bravehearts like her were very few in the Congress movement. The party's leadership was dominated by the followers of sanatana, and they overshadowed the true loyalists. There are several such examples that include Bharathi and VOC, Puducherry Subbiah and many others. Moovalurar was no exception. When she heard that Gandhi was to make a visit to south India, she arranged a conference Thiruvezhundur in Mayiladuthurai and requested Gandhi to participate. Rajaji was the organizer for Gandhi's visit at that time. He responded that Gandhi would participate in the conference only if she paid ₹500. She was furious and went directly to the place where Gandhi was staying. She read out the letter of appreciation that Gandhi had sent her and asked boldly why he has refused to attend her conference. Do we need to mention that Gandhi didn't refuse? He attended the conference along with his wife, Kasturba.

Exit from Congress: In the 1920s, during a crucial period for the Congress in Tamil Nadu, Moovalurar was a frontline leader. She was considered to be the shining star working for the cause of women. Many Congress leaders adopted an apparently moderate and conservative view in their response to social evils like untouchability, the devadasi system, child marriage and widow remarriage. However, she realized that

Hindu superstitions were the root cause of the degradation of the community. She fiercely campaigned for uprooting the sanatana ideals in order to eradicate social evils.

The sanatana followers were irate that a woman had campaigned so strongly against the apocalyptic tide. So the brahmin sanatanas who wielded power in the Congress sought to devour the entire movement. That it was impossible to fight these powers was revealed in the Kanchipuram conference in 1925. Following this, E V R Periyar left the Congress. Along with him, people like Singaravelar, Ramanathan and Moovalurar also left.

5

Self-Respect Protests in Women's Perspective

Many of the biographical accounts state that the reason for Moovalurar's exit from the Congress is unknown. But her activities in the Congress were strongly rooted in social reforms. In particular, her uncompromising protest for abolishing the devadasi system deeply unsettled the principles of sanatana. This was an era when there was a life and death struggle within the Congress between progressive thinkers and conservatives. Periyar left the Congress only because he questioned the hegemony of the sanatana power. Moovalurar not only followed him but continued to support and work with him for the Self-Respect Movement for 25 years.

In 1920, Gandhi started the second Civil Disobedience movement. Alongside, he escalated his protests against untouchability. The eradication of untouchability, however, remained a convenient facade for many Congress leaders. They were double-faced in paying lip service to the cause of untouchability even while retaining their discriminatory tendencies. This was not the case with grassroot level workers in the party who fought relentlessly against untouchability and were even willing to face imprisonment.

When Moovalurar was in the Congress many important protests took place. The Vaikom protest by Periyar happened during this period. In Kerala, people belonging to backward communities were not allowed to set foot in the streets where upper castes lived. Vaikom represented the worst of this degradation, and the protesters demanded the right for Dalits to walk on the streets. This was followed by the Gurukulam protest in Cheran Mahadevi. This was an important event which precipitated the split in the Congress. A national centre was started in Cheran Mahadevi by Va Ve Subramania Iyer. In this residential school, started on behalf of the Congress, food was served separately to the brahmin students and the others. Also, the living quarters and places of worship were different. Everywhere, clearly defined caste based discrimination between brahmins and shudras was strictly followed. When this came to light, EVR condemned it strongly. But Iyer and the brahmins held their ground, and because of this, the question of untouchability remained a mere eyewash in the Congress.

At the same time, EVR tried hard to bring in the reservation of posts in the Congress. Till then, only brahmins enjoyed the privilege of government jobs. EVR's request to the Congress was to reserve jobs for other communities and provide representation and quotas for them in government jobs. Between 1920 and 1924, EVR repeatedly tried to pass this motion in the Congress meetings. But the Congress leadership adopted many strategies and ploys to thwart them.

Kanchipuram Conference

The famous 1925 Kanchipuram conference in which EVR left the Congress took place in November of that year. Thiru V Ka was the leader of the conference. Periyar tried to propose a resolution for reservation in the conference but Thiru Vi Ka did not grant him permission to do so. 'There is no use for non-Brahmins from the Congress; from now on it's my job to vanquish the Congress.' EVR openly said, and left the meeting. Important workers of the Congress like Ramanathan, Samy Chidambaran, Moovalurar and many others left with him.

EVR convened a meeting of non-brahmins in a place very close to where the Congress meeting had happened. Everyone who left with EVR attended that meeting. It was clear that the split in the Congress was the result of the ideological conflicts that had simmered for a long time. It was these that led Moovalurar and other prominent supporters also to leave.

The idea of self-respect now spread like wildfire across Tamil Nadu. Everyday there were protests; every month had a conference; every town had a magazine, the Self-Respect Movement gained considerable momentum. Keeping up with these developments, EVR and Moovalurar travelled across Tamil Nadu together and made whirlwind trips. EVR strongly opposed the brahmins and continued to campaign intensely against their caste prejudice. During this time, in 1926, the Justice Party was trounced in the Assembly elections. The Justice Party leaders viewed the defeat as their death knell signalling the end of their political careers. But EVR rekindled their work. He convened a non-brahmin conference meeting in December in Madurai. V O Chidamabaranar joined this meeting and this helped to energise the followers. Those who had felt thwarted by the sanatana powers were now rejuvenated. Congress leaders had sought to break the Justice Party but this was averted.

Self-Respect Propaganda Conference

After two years of continuous campaigning, EVR was able to start the Self-Respect Movement in Tamil Nadu in 1927. His campaigns took the entire region by storm and the efforts of the self-respecters resulted in the first Self-Respect Movement conference in Chengalpet in February, 1929. This was followed by a spate of conferences all over Tamil Nadu. Leaders like EVR, Kuthoosi Gurusamy, Samy Chidambaran, A Ponnambalanar, KV Azhagar Samy, AS Arunachalam, Murugappa and SV Lingam took part in many campaigns. Moovalurar also campaigned extensively. In the Congress, she was the only woman to work and tour tirelessly in Tamil Nadu in the early stages of the movement.

During this time, EVR and his comrades travelled to Russia and other countries. This was an important phase in EVR's political life. When he travelled overseas in 1929-32 Moovalurar wrote numerous articles in *Kudiarasu*. When Periyar returned from his Russian trip, there was more clarity in his political perspective where socialist and communist thoughts now combined with the self-respect ideology. He stated that in order to achieve self-respect, Tamilians required economic and political freedom. He decided to announce this as a self-respect movement agenda as well. A meeting to formulate and draft the proclamation of ideals took place at his residence in Erode. This is called the 'Erode Path'. EVR, M Singaravelar, P Jeevanandam, Kuthoosi Gurusamy, Samy Chidambaran, Ramanathan and Moovalurar participated in the meeting. She played a vital role in the formulation of the Self-Respect Movement manifesto.

Self-Respect Marriages

Moovalurar's contribution towards the conduct of self-respect marriages in Tamil Nadu was significant. Her speeches at marriage halls were thought provoking. Since she was proficient in Sanskrit, she would chant the mantras in Sanskrit and also explain them in Tamil. She would also point out how the Sanskrit mantras were anti-women. This led to more awareness among the population and also resulted in more people opting for self-respect marriages.

Self-respect marriages took place in different forms such as weddings without the rituals, inter-caste, inter-religious marriages as well as widow remarriage. Marriages like those of Kunjitham–Gurusamy, Sivakami–Chidambaran, Annapoorani–Rathinasabapathy, Neelavathi–Rama Subramaniam, Murugappa-Maragathavalli, created the templates for reformist and self-respect ideology. Many of these took place because of the efforts, and under the leadership of Moovalurar. She conducted more than 80 weddings. The incidents that took place at marriages of Kunjitham-Gurusamy, Sivakami-Chidambaranar and Murugappa-Margathavalli were interesting and have been described in the Appendix.

Prohibition of the Devadasi System Act

Dr Muthulakshmi Reddy worked to pass the bill to prevent the dedication of women as devadasis. However, conservative Congressmen opposed the move. Deerar Sathyamurthy played an important role. Under his leadership, the conservatives opposed the resolution brought by Muthulakshmi. Those who supported the devadasi system argued that if the system did not continue, it would lead to the degradation of the cultural values of India. Moovalurar advised Muthulakshmi Reddy to respond thus: 'So far, women of our households have preserved Indian culture, now please permit your women to don the role for some time.' Only after Muthulakshmi Reddy put forward this argument, were the sanatana vadins silenced.

In contrast, there was complete support for this bill from the leaders of the self-respect movement and the Justice Party. In this, the support by EVR and Moovalurar was significant. Some important letters were exchanged by Muthulakshmi Reddy and Moovalurar regarding this matter. In one, the latter emphasized the need to eradicate the devadasi system even in the remote villages. At the same time, she pointed out how difficult it was to undertake this mammoth task. For instance, she pointed out that when a devadasi decided to break free from the system, she was in danger of being ostracised by the local community in villages. Therefore, it was important to provide a clause in the Devadasi Probihition Bill for this eventuality. Finally, the bill was passed in 1929.

Destroying Gandhi's Letter: After Moovalurar became involved with the Self-Respect Movement, she did not even think about the Congress. She had great respect for Gandhi but after joining the movement she forgot Gandhi along with the Congress.

'When I was deeply involved with the banning of the devadasi system, Gandhiji wrote a letter of appreciation to me. I used to offer prayers to it. After I left the Congress, I forgot not only the letter but Gandhiji himself! What's to be done!' (*Murasoli* Pongal issue 1956).

> On 27.03.1933, the Pudukottai royal court conducted a conference of the Sengunthar community. His (EVR's) speech strongly contested religious laws, belief in god

> and superstitions. Further, he also highlighted how men had forced the devadasi system on women in the name of religion and belief in god. He also pointed out how among the dedicated women, only members of a few castes were forced into prostitution. These views were many times more revolutionary than the criticism Ammaiyar had put forward while she was in the Congress. This helped Moovalur Ammaiyar understand how religion and subjugation of women were interrelated. (*Periyar's 111th Birthday Souvenir* 1989)

Following this, in 1936, she wrote and published a novel on the devadasi system named *Dasigalin Mosa Valai* or *Mathi Petra Minor*. The novel was based on her autobiographical experience and was aimed at creating awareness among devadasis. It was written in a racy style.

Protest Against the imposition of Hindi

As a result of her untiring work for social causes, Moovalurar became weak and frail. She aged quickly because she was unable to lead a healthy life as she had no material wealth, although party workers referred to her as 'grand dame'.

In the Dravidian movement, anti-Hindi protests mark a milestone. This event also enabled Dravidian politics to take root in Tamil Nadu. Moovalurar completely immersed herself in this protest. The anti-Hindi march took place for 42 days from Uraiyur in Trichy to Chennai. She walked the entire distance of 577 miles and addressed 87 public meetings. It is noteworthy that she was the only woman to take part in the protest march. 'With greying hair and feeble gait, the nearly 60-year old lady walked in support of Tamil language for more than six weeks.' (*Thaiyar Kalai* 1959).

In the same year, on 13 November 1938, the Tamil Nadu Women's conference took place in Chennai. The exclusive conference was held in a makeshift tent and was an important milestone in the women's Self-Respect Movement. Moovalurar worked hard to make the conference a success. It was only after this meeting that a 'Magalir Mandram' (Women's Assembly) was formed. Many women entered the public sphere after this. The day after the conference, there was a massive anti-Hindi protest in Chennai. Moovalurar, Dharmambal, Pattammal, Malarmugathammaiyar and Seethammal protested in front of a school, were arrested and sentenced to six months in Vellore prison. When they were released, many women didn't have the money to travel back to their homes. Moovalurar sold her gold chain and safely sent them home. After this, she never wore any gold ornaments till her death.

6

Femininity is Forever

There was some stagnation in the Self-Respect Movement as well. The number of Rao Bahadurs, zamindars and well-educated members in it increased. Members from the lower rung of society, protesters and loyalists were sidelined and neglected. Many who joined the movement after Moovalurar were recognized but she was ignored. Without the social status and education, her name is not found anywhere. Her body and mind withered because of this. In 1944, the Dravidar Kazhagam was started. Moovalurar began working with renewed enthusiasm once again. She became a pillar of the Dravidar Kazhagam. 'She was the first brave mother who spoke on the Dravidar Kazhagam platform.' (*Kalaimandram* issue—17.04.1954). Even this didn't last. Differences of opinion emerged, although the underlying reasons for these are not known. In the commemorative issue on the 111th birthday of Periyar (1989), there was a detailed essay on her. After praising her life and works, the writer concluded: 'We need to view the limitations in her thought and action against the context of the limitations in the self-respect and Dravida movements.' What were the limitations in these two movements? Who controlled them? These are issues that need research. What is clear, however, is that even in the movement for which she gave her heart and soul for 35 years, she did not get any recognition.

Honesty at Heart: Moovalurar's biggest strength was her honesty. She would speak openly and candidly to anyone. She would work for a lifetime to keep her word. She never hesitated to voice her thoughts even to EVR.

> One day Periyar asked me to find an alliance for Gurusamy. I informed him that there's a girl who has studied till her BA, but Gurusamy does not have any property, how can I search for a bride? Since Periyar promised to give some work on the magazine *Revolt* and some of his property, I arranged to have Gurusamy married to Kunjitham. However, within a short time, Periyar removed him from the job.
>
> I went and asked why Periyar had gone back on his promise and what would happen to them. I told him angrily that since both are educated, they will somehow manage and then I came home. Today I have become the enemy of Ayya but what about them…? (*Murasoli* Pongal issue 1956, p.54)

'In Ammaiyar's speech, truth and justice prevailed. Even though her words tasted bitter to men, they couldn't refute them.' (*Kalaimandram* 17.04.1954, p.20).

Periyar's Successor: In 1949, the Dravidar Kazhagam split and the DMK was formed. The main reason that was put forward was the marriage of EVR and Maniammai. While explaining the necessity to marry, EVR said, 'No one is competent to carry forward the movement after me.' To this, Moovalurar responded, 'Does it mean that even I am not qualified? Why can't you name me your heir?'

When she left the Dravidar Kazhagam along with Anna, she joined the DMK and worked very hard even at the age of 70. Despite this, it is difficult to say that she was satisfied. A few years after the DMK was formed, Moovalurar had gone to a meeting in Manapparai. After the meeting while she was resting, there was a telegram from Anna. In it, he had requested her to be the chief guest for a drama in which he acted. She was ecstatic and kept repeating: 'I have worked so long for the party but I have never been asked to chair any function.' TKS, who was at the event, confirmed that she repeated this phrase several times. This shows how deeply the indifference she faced afftected her.

Last Days: The last years of Moovalurar's life were spent at Mayiladuthurai. She and Suyambu Pillai had a son, Chellappa. In 1947, Chellappa opened a store near the railway station, 'Shop Chellappa'. He also built a house in Kaveri Nagar and lived there. In her old age, Moovalurar spent most of her time in the Kaveri Nagar home. Even though she felt dejected at the neglect she had faced, her passion for work never diminished She worked as an honorary magistrate at the Mayiladuthurai court. The Sittharkadu market which happened on Saturdays was very popular. Every week she would go there and collect donations. She helped poor children to get educated with this money. Wherever she found destitute women, she would bring them home to look after them and then she would find a safe place for them. She considered this a sacred duty. Mayura Lodge, a place near the railway station, was very popular. Many of the VIPs in Mayiladuthurai made it a point to have their morning and evening coffee there. Even to this day, senior citizens recall how Moovalurar would walk from home with a walking stick to Mayura Lodge to drink coffee.

Across from Mayura Lodge was Kanakasabhai Nadar's house. Often, after her coffee, she would go across to have a conversation with him on social and national issues. The Hindu newspaper would arrive and Nadar's daughter-in-law, Meenambal Vellaithambi, would read it out to Ammaiyar who was not fluent in English but understood it well enough. Meenambal Vellaithambi, now in her 70s, recalls:

> First Ammaiyar would ask me to read the headlines. Then she would choose the news items she wanted to hear about in detail. I was newly-married when I met her. She was already old. I did not know much about her political activities but she had spoken to me on many occasions about the devadasi system. For men, in those times, going to a dasi's house was like chewing betel leaf and spitting it out.

As she grew older, her eyesight worsened. Despite this, she took care of her routine activities on her own and also did some odd jobs. She would help to thread the beads sold at her son's shop. She did this as a hobby. Despite her poor eyesight, she would thread the beads by having different coloured beads in small cups on either side. This was mentioned by Kaliyamurthy, the present owner of Chellapa Store who had worked there earlier. After Moovalurar passed away in 1962, her son moved to Chennai along with his family. The store he set up is still there but for the last 50 years it has been run by Kaliyamurthy. Moovalurar's son was a good musician and was known as 'All India Radio fame Sangeetha Vidwan'. He passed away a while ago and his son now lives in Chennai, with the next generation in America.

Anna Award: For her public life spanning over 50 years, the only recognition Moovalurar received in her own lifetime was the award given by Annadurai on behalf of the DMK. Annadurai decided to honour those who contributed to the cause of the Self-Respect Movement. The very first name that he chose was that of Moovalurar. This award was presented in 1956 and it was the first and last award presented on behalf of the DMK. In his speech at the award function, Annadurai said, 'We have given this award—on a wooden plank embedded with a piece of silver—according to our financial condition. However, by presenting this award, we have surrendered our hearts to her.' In subsequent years, Annadurai remained affectionate and fond of Moovalurar. At the award function he compared her to Annie Beasant. But he was also aware of her sense of dejection. He said, 'Moovalur Ramamirtham Ammaiyar has become physically weak. Even though she remains mentally strong, to a certain extent, a kind of fatigue has set in.'

No honour or award was given to her by the central government. People like Muthulakshmi Reddy, Ambujammal and Neelavathi Ramasubramaniam, who worked with her and after her, all received government awards and honours. But despite the fact that she worked as a single woman, she carried bales of khadi on her head, received a letter of appreciation from Gandhi for her work towards the rehabilitation of women, the post-independence Indian government completely forgot her. Perhaps this was because she did not belong to the brahmin caste nor was she dependent on them for her livelihood. She did not hail from a zamindar or Rao Bahadur lineage. She was not a political opportunist. She was born in a caste which had enslaved women for over 2000 years. She fought to liberate them and succeeded. She worked for social reforms and national independence. She witnessed many social reform laws being enacted in her own lifetime. In a sense, that was her lifetime achievement and greatest honour.

Moovalur Ramamirtham Ammaiyar Marriage Assistance Scheme: A higher secondary school in Moovalur has been named after Moovalurar. When Kalaignar assumed office for the third time as Chief Minister (1989–1991) he announced a marriage assistance scheme for young girls in her name. For poor girls who had studied till the 8th standard, a sum of ₹5,000 was given as marriage assistance. When Jayalalitha assumed office (1991-1996) this scheme was shelved. When Kalaignar came back to power (1996-2001), the scheme was revived and the amount was increased to ₹10,000. When Jayalalitha assumed office, the scheme once again went into cold storage. Later, when Karunanidhi formed the government, he announced during the swearing in ceremony that the amount would be increased to ₹15,000 for the Moovalur Ramamirtham Ammaiyar Marriage Assistance Scheme revival. It is heartening that the government led by Jayalalitha has continued the scheme. Many people in Moovalur have requested that the government convert Moovalur's house into a memorial.

Women's Rights: Yesterday, Today, Tomorrow: The position of women has improved. Earlier, a wife could not question even if the husband had many mistresses. But this is not possible now. A husband cannot take a mistress at will. The wife can declare her unwillingness to live with him and demand her share of property. If a man remarries when his wife is alive, that marriage is nullified and will attract a penalty and jail term. A man cannot refer to his wife in derogatory terms such as 'adi' or subject her to violence. If she informs the court that he uses derogatory and abusive language, the courts will demand an explanation and impose a fine and the husband is forced to apologize.

A wife can even take it further and object. 'He smokes beedis and they are foul smelling. I don't wish to live with him.' Today, women have an equal share in their father's property. If a father has one daughter and one son, and property of worth a lakh of rupees, it has to be shared equally between them. If she's smart, she can refuse to let the last rites happen till the property is shared. Today, we find women getting all kinds of education and jobs like men.

> Currently, a woman, Mrs Lourdu Ammal is a minister. There are women in high offices like collectors and lawyers. We have worked tirelessly for women to reach this status. We have faced severe hardships and taunts. The social reforms that we have worked towards have now been enacted as laws. Can there be a better reward to make us happy? You need to remember the extent of our courage and determination. (Periyar's speech in Valikandapuram on 26.08.1959 and published in *Viduthalai* magazine 31.08.1959)

Fascist and conservative powers are rearing their ugly heads once again. Using the chinks in the armour of these laws, women are prevented from taking full advantage of the laws. Recent times have seen a rise in violence against women. Thus, the battle begun by Periyar and Moovalurar appears to have ended, but the truth is, it still continues.

7

Education – Courtesy Grandma

Moovalurar's grandson, Selvaraj, was an important presence in her life as she grew into old age. At 75 now, he shared his memories of his grandmother in an interview on 19.12.2006. He described how Suyambu Pillai and Moovalurar had two sons and one daughter. The older son and daughter passed away tragically from an unknown disease. This was a turning point in Moovalurar's life. Up until this time she had been a staunch believer but now, furious that god had not shown any compassion, she completely gave up on her belief.

Chellappa, her youngest son, was not particularly interested in studying. So he gave up by the time he got to the fifth standard. He was more interested in music, and took after his father, Suyambu. In the gurukula tradition, he stayed with Kumbakonam Fiddle Rajamanickam Pillai as his disciple and learnt music. He started giving solo concerts. Since he was naturally gifted with a wonderful voice, he performed for All India Radio, Trichy and came to be known as Radio celebrity Moovalur Chellappa.

Even though Moovalurar was a prominent leader in the Self-Respect Movement, her domestic life was spent in poverty.

Selvaraj states that in his growing years, he has never seen sweets and delicacies being prepared.

> Grandfather Suyambu Pillai had some land in Keeranur near Sikkil. The rice we got from here was our staple. Even though rice was available, we didn't have other groceries. She would make sambar with brinjals grown in the garden. She didn't waste even the stalks and scrambled them into the curry. She was thrifty. Since our family had been ostracised, we didn't have much of an income. Grandpa Suyambu Pillai taught music to students in Mayavaram and nearby places. Appa earned a little through concerts but that was not a steady income.
>
> If Paati came to know about devadasis in the neighbourhood, she would befriend them. If she came to know about the dedication of girls, she would talk to them secretly and help them escape from the house at night. Before that, she would lodge a complaint in the police station under the Prohibition of Devadasi Act. Then, she would make arrangements for the girl to stay at Avvai Illam in Chennai which was run by Muthulakshmi Reddy. Her next job was to find a suitable, groom and get the girl married.

This phase was important in Moovalurar's campaigns within the Self-Respect Movement. She would share all details of matters discussed in meetings with her grandson.

> She would tell me about the places she visited and people she met and it was like a story. And she told me about her own struggles, the evils of the devadasi system, the cruelty of the zamindars, the heads of mutts, and affluent men. Because of this I was drawn to the Self-Respect Movement at an early age. She took me along with her during my

holidays. Later, when I was caught up with my studies and my job, she would take Mayavaram Kitappa—she needed someone with her as she was growing old. Later Kitappa became MLA from the Mayavaram constituency.

In 1935, she wrote the novel *Dasigalin Mosa Valai* or *Mathi Petra Minor*. When the Cauvery was without an inflow of water, she would lie on her stomach and write. Then I would play collecting shells. There were many thazhambu bushes on the banks of the Cauvery. One day, when she was writing, a snake climbed onto her. But she didn't see it. Thinking it was a little stick she dusted it off and continued writing.

Ammaiyar's beloved husband Suyambu Pillai passed away in 1936. After that, Chellappa reduced the number of concerts he performed. He started Shop Chellappa, a fancy store near Mayiladuthurai railway station. Since many railway employees lived there, the business picked up well and income increased. Ammaiyar's family moved to a house in Vaduga street to be close to the shop. Later Chellappa worked hard and bought a house and also a piece of land in Cauvery Nagar. He also bought a premises for his shop.

He said, 'In 1948, the Dravidar Kazhagam conducted a conference in Saakkottai near Kumbakonam. During the conference, Annadurai and DV Narayanasamy acted in a play entitled "Hindu Kingdom envisioned by Shivaji." Paati played the role of the hero's mother. She wore the sacred ash on her forehead. That was the only time I saw her do that.'

In the meantime, Moovalurar had signed a surety for a loan taken by Kumbakonam Chinnayya Pillai, who was unable to repay, and there was talk of initiating action against her. She was forced to sell the land she had bought near Keeranur to repay the loan.

During this time, Selvaraj completed his schooling. He had scored very high marks in the final examination and he wanted to study further. Sympathetic to her grandson's desire, even though she did not like asking for favours, Moovalurar took him to Annadurai. Anna took Selvaraj to the then Vice Chancellor of Chidambaram Annamalai University Mr Manavala Ramanujam, and he got admission into the Engineering College. In those days, it was rare for backward class people to be able to get entry to engineering courses. Moovalurar sold her house in Moovalur for her grandson's education. Selvaraj also mentioned that on the days when his father was in town he would spend time with her. Chellappa often went to Bengaluru to buy things like ribbon rolls, coloured beads, etc. that he needed. Selvaraj said,

> Paati used to help Appa cut the ribbons and thread the beads into necklaces. She would help a lot and also get a salary. At home, she would buy coconuts, dry them and extract oil and sell. She supported the household with these earnings and also used the money for her travels. She never asked Appa any money for her expenses. Like thatha, Appa never opposed or supported Paati's public service. He would remain silent because it brought back memories of the poverty he faced in his younger days. Thererfore, he never permitted me to join the movement or take part in politics.

When Selvaraj completed his engineering in 1954, he got a government job in the highways department. The same year, he got married to Sokkayi Nachiyar, who was the daughter of Sivagiri Zamindar. Her mother belonged to the Isai Vellala community and was not the legal wife of the zamindar. However, Sivagiri Zamindar announced that Sokkayi Nachiyar was his daughter. He was the brother of Vellaithuraichi Nachiyar, who published the novel, *Dasigalin Mosa Valai*. Moovalurar had remained with her grandson from the time he got married till 1961. Selvaraj had two sons and a daughter. His daughter was born two months after Moovalurar died, and he named her Rani Ramamirtham in his grandmother's memory.

Except Selvaraj, the other grandchildren did not want information about them to be published. They avoided any meeting by stating that what is available in the novel is more than enough. But they did say this: 'She used to come and go. This is how we thought of her when we were young. We didn't realize that she was a towering personality. We only thought of her as an old lady at home.' One of Ammaiyar's great granddaughters voiced these words with a lot of regret.

Moovalurar – Suyambu Pillai – Grandson Selvaraj

Annexures

1

Self-Respect Marriages

The Marriage of Kunjitham and Kuthoosi Gurusamy: Within the first five or six years of the launch of self-respect marriages across Tamil Nadu, the wedding of Kunjitham and Gurusamy took place and shook the entire state. When EVR requested Moovalurar to find an educated bride for Gurusamy, she identified Kunjitham. On 8 December, 1929 at Erode, Kunjitham, who belonged to the lower caste of Isai Vellala and Gurusamy, who belonged to the upper caste of Mudaliars were married in a ceremony conducted by Self-Respecters under the leadership of Periyar. This was the first self-respect marriage conducted after the movement was launched. This was also an inter-caste marriage. It was discussed far and wide in Tamil Nadu. Kunjitham broke the stereotype of a docile bride. She delivered a short speech that took everyone by surprise with its power. She said,

> Indian women were treated like animals thus far because women were not given education by parents. There was a time when it was believed that women cannot compete with men in terms of physical strength and intelligence. That

> time has long passed. If the status of Indian women has to improve, they need to have the urge to study. In order to compete at a global level, there should be good support at the familial level. (*Kuthoosi Gurusamy* p.193)

Kunjitham received widespread appreciation for her views. In later years, she went on to become an eminent educationist.

The Marriage of Sivakami and Samy Chidambaran: Within the next five months, another revolutionary marriage took place between Samy Chidambaran and Sivagami. 45 years after the event, TV Meikandar wrote in detail about it in the special issue on the women's conference in *Kazhagakural.* Since this wedding was very significant, the extract is reproduced in full.

> Sivagami Ammaiyar belonged to the padayachi community. Since her father was engaged in the textile business, he took the surname Pillai. Samy Chidambaran belonged to the Malayaman subsect of the Saiva Udayar community. Their marriage was reformist, inter-caste and widow remarriage rolled into one.
>
> Sivagami Ammaiyar's father, Kuppusamy Pillai, was the telegram master in the railways. After his father, Appasamy Pillai's demise, he left the job and became involved in his father's wholesale business of silk garments. By the age of 30, he became rich. He worked as a Member of the Kumbakonam City Council and an honorary magistrate. He was also a prominent member of the Justice party and became close to Periyar. He was the first subscriber of *Kudiarasu* magazine. On reading the articles in this magazine, he began to follow atheistic principles. He stopped performing the death ceremony, wearing the sacred ash and rudraksha beads. He stopped his family,

including Sivagami Ammaiyar, from attending any temple festivities. He had five daughters and no son. He had two wives and Sivagami Ammaiyar was the eldest daughter of his second wife.

Sivagami Ammaiyar got married for the first time when she was 11. The groom, Ramasamy, was a BA student at Pachaiyappa's College at the time. He was a widower and his wife had died during childbirth. He was a wealthy mirasidar. Sadly, within a few months of marrying Sivagami Ammaiyar, he died due to typhoid.

Sivagami Ammaiyar's father asked her to remove the thali and hand it over to the groom's family. He informed them that she would continue to wear flowers and kumkum and that she should not be forced into any rituals. Her in-laws were not happy about this and there was an altercation and he brought Sivagami back home on the 16th day after her husband's demise. Her father-in-law understood her plight and gave her permission to follow her father's wishes. Even when she attained the age of 18, she didn't don the widow's garb. However, the family didn't permit her to attend any public events. So, her mother also stayed away. The family engaged women tutors and educated her at home and also held classes in Tamil, English and tailoring. She studied till the 9th grade.

Kuppusamy Pillai began to think of remarriage after reading some articles in *Kudiarasu.* He made Sivagami Ammaiyar and her mother read those articles as well. His aim was to kindle some radical thoughts in them. Since he started attending Periyar's meetings, over a period of time, he became convinced about remarriage.

Kuppusamy Pillai arranged to have Moovalurar speak to Sivagami Ammaiyar and her mother. This was because of her commitment to women's liberation and her

> active promotion of reformist and intercaste marriages. Subramaniam was a neighbour who lived some ten houses away and who had educated his widowed daughter till graduation as far back as 1905. Later, she chose her own partner. Subramaniam often visited Kuppusamy Pillai's family and he would advise Kuppusamy to not confine his daughter but to do something. Pillai listened to him and tried to convince Sivagami Ammaiyar's mother who was concerned that this may damage the marriage prospects of her other daughters. Five years passed without anything happening and Sivagami turned 18.

When he came back from the conferences organized by Periyar, Kuppusamy Pillai told his wife that Periyar had asked him several times what he had decided. He had also suggested, through Moovalurar, many prospective grooms: Murugappa, Janaka Sankara Kannappar, Rama, Subramaniam and Samy Chidambaran. Kuppusamy Pillai chose Samy Chidambaran. He sent his friend Subramania Pillai who was also the Secretary of the Self-Respect Movement in Kumbakonam, to meet Chidambaran, who was then working as Tamil teacher at Raja Madam, to obtain his consent.

Kuppusamy Pillai wanted to finalise the alliance in the presence of Periyar and at a time Samy Chidambaran was in Erode. He wrote to Periyar, and Periyar suggested he come right away. A telegram was then sent by Periyar to Samy Chidambaran who was in Madurai preparing textbooks, to come immediately to Erode. Once there, he was asked, in the presence of Kuppusamy Pillai, Periyar, S Ramanathan and Mayavaram Ganesan, whether he would be open to the alliance. Samy Chidambaram said that he would agree only after meeting the bride in person and obtaining her consent.

One week later, Chidambaran sent a letter by post and came to Kumbakonam. Subramania Pillai, Moovalurar, Sudalai Muthu Nadar and Chinnathambi Nadar accompanied him. Sivagami Ammaiyar was asked to bring a plate of sugar candy to everyone by way of the 'bride viewing' ceremony. Chidambaran wanted to see the bride's handwriting. Kuppusamy Pillai showed him the notebook in which she had written lyrics of songs. Moovalurar asked him to request her to write something then and there. Sivagami Ammaiyar wrote 'Women's liberation is the real spirit of the nation's independence.'

'We haven't obtained her acceptance,' said Samy Chidambaram.

Moovalurar and Subramania Pillai asked Sivagami Ammaiyar to come and sit with them and told Samy Chidambaran to ask her whatever he wanted. Samy Chidambaran asked his prospective bride. 'I earn ₹45 and my job is not permanent. If I lose the job I may have carry headloads at the railway station. I don't have any property. You belong to a wealthy family. We may not have an affluent life. If it's alright by you, we can marry.'

Moovalurar and Subramania Pillai laughed out aloud and said, 'You are scaring her.'

Subramania Pillai had already highlighted Samy Chidambaran's virtues and character and given the textbooks written by him to Sivagami Ammaiyar. She shyly uttered her assent and ran inside.

Kuppusamy Pillai and Samy Chidambaran wrote to Periyar about their acceptance of the alliance. Periyar replied that the marriage could take place in May when Samy Chidambaran's school would have summer holidays. It was decided that on 30 April 1930, Samy Chidambaran would travel from Raja Madam to Erode, Sivagami Ammaiyar would travel along with Moovalurar and Subramania Pillai.

Sivagami Ammaiyar's mother bid her daughter farewell with tears of joy. Her father accompanied her to the railway station. Kuppusamy Pillai who was conversing alone with Samy Chidambaran burst into tears like a child. Sivagami Ammaiyar also broke down. The wedding party which left Kumbakonam at 4 pm reached Erode at 1 pm the next day.

Periyar and S Ramanathan were talking in Periyar Maligai and didn't know about their arrival. The bride and groom walked in front and the others followed. Periyar and Ramanathan were shocked when they saw an honest and upright gentleman like Samy Chidambaran with an unknown woman. Subramanya Pillai and Moovalurar who came behind started clapping and laughing. Only then did Periyar and Ramanathan realize that it was the bride. Moovalurar asked the bride to take Periyar's blessings and Sivagami Ammaiyar fell at his feet.

'What's all this! Ramamirthamma.... Why don't you keep still?' Periyar asked.

Samy Chidambaran put his hand on Ramanathan's shoulder.

The place was new for Sivagami Ammaiyar and she felt shy and tears welled up.

'Nagai, Nagai...please come here,' Periyar called out loudly.

Nagammaiyar came out, embraced the bride and took her inside. Since it was already 2'o clock, she asked the bride to bathe and eat her lunch.

The wedding was on 5 May 1930. The arrangements were done at lightning speed. Invitations were printed and Periyar himself signed and sent them out. He insisted that he would bear the entire expenses of the wedding. Invitations were sent to important comrades of the Self-Respect Movement as well as to people in places where self-respect groups operated. The invitation was also published in newspapers like *Kudiarasu, Kumaran* and *Dravidan* in 4 May edition.

Invitations were not sent to Sivagami Ammaiyar's relatives. Similarly, Samy Chidambaran did not send invitations to his family. He sent to his friends and students. Till the marriage happened, his family had no information about it. This was how this marriage took place.

Marriage of Maragathavalli and Murugappa: The marriage of Murugappa and Maragathavalli was a unique one which questioned the status quo. This was also an inter-caste and widow remarriage.

During the Self-Respect Movement conference that took place in Pattukottai under the leadership of Pattukottai Alagirisamy, there was an interesting debate about widow remarriage. There was an important reason for this. It was no surprise that Moovalurar took part in the debate. A young widow named Maragathavalli came as a spectator to the conference. She sent a message to Moovalurar on a small bit of paper:

'You have conducted many widow remarriages. Can you conduct my marriage because I am also a young widow?'

The next day, a young man named Murugappa, who was the editor of *Kumaran* magazine, gave a passionate speech about widow remarriage. Moovalurar, who was sitting in the front row threw a question at him:

'All's fine with the rhetoric, comrade Murugappa. Will young men like you exhibit the same spirit in your deeds as you do with words? Are you ready to share your life with a widow?'

Murugappa retorted.

'We do what we say. We consider it an insult that you think of us as empty vessels.'

'If that's the case, please ask such young men in this gathering to raise their hands.'

'I'll first raise my hand,' said Murugappa and this was followed by many raised hands.

'Dear Madam, you cast an aspersion on us but how many women have you moulded to enter into such revolutionary marriage?' he asked in return.

'Mr Murugappa, times have changed. Young women today are mature and willing enough to enter into inter-caste marriage and widow remarriage. If there are grooms who come forward, I will show them the brides.'

'Fine. Here's the first groom—I am ready. Please bring the bride,' said Murugappa.

In the next instant, 'Here's the bride,' said Moovalurar and asked the young woman seated beside her to get up. She astonished the entire gathering.

In the meeting podium itself, the bride and the groom were introduced and the wedding was announced. In later days, Maragathavalli assumed charge as editor of *Widow Remarriage (Maathar Marumanam)* magazine.

These two weddings exemplify Moovalur Ammaiyar's proactive and daring efforts to bring about revolutionary marriages.

2

Dasigalin Mosa Valai or Mathi Pertra Minor

In 1936, Moovalur Ramamirtham Ammaiyar wrote about the life of devadasis, and the things that helped them break free in a novel entitled, Dasigalin Mosa Valai. *After 65 years, it has been reprinted.*

The novel portrays two devadasis popularly called Kamalapuram dasis and shows how they extort money from affluent minors and zamindars. It depicts, through sudden twists and interesting anecdotes in the plot, how one minor had a change of heart and how he saved other such men. Natarajan who got cheated by the devadasi works as their mama or pimp in disguise. Another person, Gunabhushani, who refuses to be involved in the devadasi practice, marries Sivaraman of her own caste, lives in Chennai and works to eradicate the system. Together Gunabhushani, Sivaraman and mama, teach a lesson to the Kamalapuram dasis and bring about a change of heart in the Dharmapuri prince.

Even though it appears to be a propaganda story, the novel's style and description has a modern and realistic structure. Many questions arise when we consider the fact that it was a campaign tool in the Self-Respect Movement and yet it hasn't had a complete review even after 70 years. It is a matter of surprise that the Dravidian movement which had emphasized drama and films neglected this literary work. Secondly, this work has not gained enough attention among literary scholars. It is obvious that the character Gunabhushani is modelled on Moovalur Ammaiyar. A representative extract from the novel is presented here.

Naivete that refuses to learn a lesson

Mama went to Kamalapuram dasi's house. Hiding their annoyance, they welcomed him.

'Mama, how come it took so long for you to return with the jewellery?' asked Kantha. 'You have a lot of young ladies to look after. Perhaps, you forgot us because of them. What can you do? Their wiles and charms must have captivated you,' she spoke banteringly and with a smile.

'I was embarrassed to meet you. A wealthy man took the money you gave. I parted with it thinking it would help you. He hasn't returned it yet. I was delayed because I couldn't face you. But don't worry,' he said.

'Mama, why do you treat us like strangers? Is there any difference in your money and mine? With your support, I can achieve anything. We were greedy and we lost everything. I have consulted the astrologer. It seems I have had the Saturn ascendant for seven and a half years. This trouble will continue for two more months. After that it will be the Sukra dasa, according to the Panchanga Iyer. Because of this Sani, even my sisters are estranged. You have come with the dasa of wealth. After all even King Nala could not escape the hold of Saturn. Oh Mama! How can I explain the troubles we faced and are still facing? Since other dasis will make fun of us, we are selling even our saris to run the household. I don't have even four annas to do a puja to Saneeswara Bhagavan.'

Mama thought to himself.

'They have still not come out of their irrational belief in horoscopes. The Lord of wealth will pour, it seems. They have grown old and with grey hair and missing teeth they plan to change the tide. Shameless harlots!'

'Kantha, don't worry. I feel sad on seeing your plight. Let Sukra dasa come at its own pace. Now, listen to me. Dharmapuri zamindar is in a good position now. He's organizing a conference in Trichy. Some lady from Chennai will be the chief guest. I have arranged for your concert. If you listen to me, you can change the tide in your favour.'

'I don't mind coming, mama, but I don't have any jewellery.'

'Don't worry about that. I will tell you a plan. Listen carefully. He may be unhappy with you. You assume the name of his wife. If he asks you for your name, tell him that you are Gnanasundari. If he asks you about your sad plight, you say that your husband was in dasi Kantha's house and that you came in search of him but didn't find him there. Since he would have come back there at some point, you stayed on there. Dasi Kantha's family forced you to take up singing and you had to oblige. Act like a true wife and he will return to you. After that, I will take care of things. It's better you don't wear ornaments. It will be more believable.'

Kantha thought that her luck had returned and that Mama was hatching a master plan. She agreed to accompany him and act accordingly. Bhoga Chintamani and Ganavathy were really worried. Mama set their minds at rest and left for Trichy.

Reception and Dinner: The entire town of Trichy wore a festive look. There were wall posters and notices all over the town announcing the arrival of Gunabhushani and Sivaraman who were well-known social reformers in Chennai. There were several 'bit notices' about the dinner reception to be hosted by Somsekhara Duraipandya Iyan in his garden retreat for the couple who had come to attend the social reform conference in Trichy. For the local people, it was a unique occasion. Usually, the annual day celebrations of the Justice Party, the Self-Respect Movement, the Congress Party, Tamil development, religious development and association meetings were held in Trichy and the leaders were well-known. But who were Gunabhushani and Sivaraman? Who was Somashekhara Duraipandian? What was the purpose of the meeting? It was also advertised that affluent zamindars, including those from Dharmapuri and Swarnapuri, would participate. They were surprised and fearful. Many had decided to be present at the dinner. The day before, festoons and arches were hung in important lanes and railway station. Gunabhushani, Sivaraman and Karunakaran arrived the next morning by the overnight 'mail' train. Kantha, Ganavathy and Bhoga Chintamani also arrived on the same train.

They were greeted by a crowd of people. Mama and Gunasekaran garlanded and welcomed Gunabhushani and her team. After this, they were taken in a motor car procession complete with a musical band. Gunabhushani and Sivaraman were ecstatic at the reception accorded to them. How can we describe Karunkaran's state of mind? Earlier, he had believed that the adoption of the devadasi livelihood by his sisters was a matter of pride. What did he feel now? By serving his dasi sisters, he was forced to even carry headloads. But by travelling with his once despised sister, he was able to ride in a car. He was pleased and lost in thoughts like these. The procession reached Somashekaran's bungalow. No one bothered about Kantha's group. They hired a horse cart and reached their allocated quarters.

A sumptuous breakfast was served to the important guests from Chennai. Then, everyone dispersed. After lunch, the

Gunabhushani-Sivaraman group rested to recover from their travel. Preparations were in full swing at Somasekaran's bungalow for the evening dinner. Guests from within and outside Trichy started arriving at Somashekara Duraipandi Iyan's bungalow from 4.30 pm. The dinner reception combined aspects of British and Indian cultures. After dinner, a certificate of appreciation was read out and presented to Gunabhushani and Sivaraman for their exemplary social service. A music concert by the Kamalapuram sisters followed. Bhoga Chintamani and team felt embarrassed and jealous of their situation. They were annoyed at Mama for arranging the concert.

'Truly Kali Kalam has arrived. So much attention for this worthless loafer. Karunakaran, who was running errands at home, has risen in stature. He is seated as an equal with the wealthy men. Sivaraman, the pauper, looks like a maharaja now. Can't recognize him,' Bhoga Chintamani complained to her daughters.

But what was the use of such complaints? The concert had to go on. Controlling their feelings, they somehow finished the concert., The guests left after confirming their presence at the conference the next day. The Kamalapuram troupe also went back.

Adding Fuel to Fire: After dinner, Mama informed Gunabhushani about the current state of affairs and explained why he had invited Kantha, and about Gnanasundari's disguise as Kantha, and Somasekharan's attitude, all of this in great detail and with clarity. He requested her to transform Somesekharan and send him to his kingdom along with Gnanasundari. Gunabhushani promised to try her best. She also planned to bring Kantha at an appropriate moment when she is conversing with Somasekharan. Gnanasundari was present during this conversation. Later, all of them went to Somasekaran's residence. On learning about her proposed visit, Somasekharan greeted her at the entrance and seated her comfortably.

Gunabhushani: I have come to discuss some matters with you. I have some doubts and would like to clarify them.

Somasekharan: I am happy and grateful for this opportunity to converse with you. Please feel free to ask me anything and I will answer to the best of my knowledge.

Gunabhushani: Who's the sister with you? Is she your wife or concubine?

Somasekharan: Earlier she was a dasi but now I look upon her as someone even more special than my wife.

Gunabhushani: What's the reason for considering her as a dasi earlier and a wife now?

Somasekharan: Since she has surrendered herself to me, I think of her as my wife.

Gunabhushani: The one who believes her husband counts as a wife and the one who doesn't, is a dasi, is that it? This is what I understand from what you are saying. Does your wife trust you? So, you have decided to accord that status to this woman?

Somasekharan: I am not bothered about her. I came here soon after our wedding. If she cared for me, she would have come in search of me.

Gunabhushani: Did you feel bad when the woman next to you, who was a dasi earlier, did not trust you and evicted you with the help of another man? Later, when she apologized, you accepted her? Suppose your wife bore the name of a dasi but was virtuous, how would you treat her? If your wife was engaged in prostitution because of her mistrust, you wouldn't mind that, I hope.

Somasekharan: You cannot speak like that. However virtuous she is, if she bears the name of a dasi, I will not accept that, and even if I am willing to accept this, the world will not do so.

Gunabhushani: Why will you not accept that? If a dasi can indulge in prostitution with many men and return as a virtuous woman and you would give her the status of a wife, why can't you treat your wife well? What is so special about dasis that is not there in wives? I seek your explanation on this.

Somasekharan: Would I have come here giving up everything, if she's not special? Do I need to list it out?

Gunabhushani: You don't need to elaborate. If this sister is Kantha, then who was the woman who performed in the concert some time back?

Somasekharan: I don't know who she is.

Gunabhushani: Shall we enquire?

When Somasekharan agreed, she signalled to Gnanasundari to hide and asked Mama to fetch Kantha. Immediately, he left and informed Kantha,

'The zamindar wants to meet you. Good fortune has arrived. He's talking with Gunabhushani but don't get scared. Looks like she'll spoil our plans. Do as I say. I'll take care of the consequences.'

Kantha was overjoyed and, believing that her luck had returned, she went with Mama to meet Somasekharan. Even though she knew Gunabhushani, she was sure that the latter would not recognize her and so she stood there, confident.

When she saw Kantha, Gunabhushani welcomed her and said, 'Come Madam. The zamindar wants to meet you. Please take a seat.'

Kantha pretended to be shy like a virtuous wife and remained standing. Since Gunabhushani understood the ploy, she requested Somasekharan to make her sit down. She sat at the edge of her seat.

'What's your native place? Please don't mistake me. Since the zamindar has a doubt, I am merely clarifying it.'

Kantha pretended to be upset and then said, in a slightly embarrassed voice, 'Madam, if my story is told, the world will laugh at me. I am the daughter of a zamindar and married to the son of a zamindar. My husband left with the dasis who performed at our marriage. I went in search of him but he was not there in the dasi's house. In the hope that he would return one day, I stayed on in their house. They wanted me to enter their profession. I refused to engage in prostitution but agreed to perform music. My name is Gnanasundari.'

Somasekharan fainted when he heard the name Gnanasundari. They managed to revive him, he was crestfallen and several thoughts crowded around in his mind.

'Ayyo! What evil times these are! I have become the cause for the fallen state of a zamindar's daughter. Having taken the identity as my wife, should she face this plight?"

Her father will commit suicide if he hears about this. As for me my community will think ill of me. A man who visits the house of dasis faces social criticism. Yet, our hearts melt on seeing them. We ignore the shame and degradation and think of them as our refuge. It's better for a man, who seeks pleasure in a dasi's house to remain unmarried. A woman who could have lived a noble life has been brought to this sad state. Men have become the cause of the fallen state of virtuous women and not the other way. What can be done now? How will I go back and rule my zamin? Even if I do, this blot will not disappear. I have betrayed Kantha. If I return with her, I will be criticized by everyone. If I tell Gnanasundari this, she will think ill of me.

Meanwhile, Gnanasundari and Gunabhushani watched silently. Then, Gunabhushani asked Somasekharan, 'Why are you looking so dejected and in deep thought? When a special woman is with you, why are you so concerned about an ordinary woman's words? You seem to be contradicting yourself.'

'Even if I am not worried, I am concerned about how my relatives and society will ridicule me.'

Then Gunabhushani whispered to him:

I doubt this woman is your wife. She would never have agreed to be roped into this profession. Even if she had reached the dasi's house in search of you, she wouldn't have stayed there. Maybe she went there because of her affection for you. A virtuous wife would never indulge in an activity that would hurt your feelings. As a zamindar's wife, your wife may have disguised herself and done daring acts which will make the world praise her but she wouldn't indulge in an act that degrades her. Even naïve women would not go to a dasi's house. Instead, they will stay at home, reconciled to their fate. If that's so for ordinary women, would a zamindarini decide to do this kind of thing? Think clearly. This is not your wife. I think she is dasi Kantha. I distrust her words. You ask her the names of her parents and parents-in-law and if she responds correctly, let her know that you have accepted Kantha as the legally wedded wife and that you have promised that her son (when born) will be the heir. Ask her to return to her father's house. I will take care of things after that.

Surprised by her words, Somsekharan said, 'You are wrong. Dasi Kantha is with me. Your statements are false. Do you think

I don't recognize her? If she is dasi Kantha, would she come in this state to the concert? Do you know how much jewellery she owns? She would have left soon after the concert. Since she's my wife, she has come without ornaments. Would Kantha's mother let her come out in public without jewels? Who do you think is with me?'

Gunabhushani pleaded. 'Please listen to me. What you see or hear may be deceptive. It's better to enquire and find the truth. If she's your wife, she won't be so knowledgeable about music. Dasis trick people and connive. You may ask why she should claim to be your wife. It is a truism that a hasty man is unthinking and a greedy man does not scrutinize. Someone who knows you, might have asked her to act. Dasis are not discerning and in their haste to make money, they may act according to the wishes of others. However much they earn, they surrender it to someone and suffer in their old age. Do you know of any dasi who has lived decently in her old age? Look closely. Don't doubt that she's not wearing jewels. Without a doubt, she is Kantha.'

Somasekharan was not convinced but he summoned the real Kantha and asked her to mention the names of her father, mother, father-in-law and mother-in-law. Kantha was flummoxed. Since she didn't know their names, she said that respect demands that she not utter the names of elders.

'Okay, out of respect you cannot utter the names of your parents-in-law. Why don't you just mention the names of your parents?

She refused.

'Why don't you to write them down?'

'Whether I say or write, it amounts to disrespecting them.'

On hearing this, Somsekharan said, 'I am Somasekharan. You leave. I consider dasi Kantha as my truly wedded wife. I have decided to name the son born to us as the heir to the zamin. I have promised her. There's no point in your waiting. You return to your father's house or anywhere. You cannot stay here.'

Kantha was shell shocked when she heard these words. 'Ayyo! I have been ruined by Mama's words. The zamindar still has affection for me. Had I told the truth, he would have chased away the fake woman and lived with me. That Mama, the great sinner, has ruined everything. What shall I do now? I'll utter the truth and put the blame on Mama. He may become interested in me then.'

She stood there, very worried. At this moment, Gunabhushani summoned Gnanasundari and made the real and fake Kantha stand next to each other. She asked Somasekharan, 'Who is the real Kantha?'

He couldn't find any difference and simply stared.

'I can't tell the difference. Please identify the real one. Hereafter, I'll follow your advice.'

Gunabhushani looked at the real Kantha and said,

'You tell your real history. The zamindar has some suspicions. If you tell the truth, you can benefit.'

Realizing that she cannot carry the pretense any more, she said, 'Madam, what I utter is the truth. It's not my fault. I am dasi Kantha. Mama asked me to act this way and I said what he told me to say. In our profession, we cannot ignore Mama's words. Since he chooses and brings the clients for us, we believe him. I trusted him now as well. Since I didn't want to live with another partner after zamindar left, I lost the wealth I had earned. I don't have anyone to support me, except the zamindar. The woman standing here is using my name to beguile him and usurp his wealth. I am the real Kantha. She has disguised herself to look like me. Don't believe her.'

Somasekharan was dazed and confused. At this juncture, Mama arrived. Gunabhushani asked him,

'The entire duty is on you. Who is the real Kantha? Please let us know.

Laughing aloud, Mama said,

'What kind of joke is this! Let's discuss all this tomorrow. I have a lot of work for the conference. Please forgive me and grant me permission to leave. I am going to the fort,' and he left.

Somasekharan was in a dilemma. Gunabhushani's information appeared confusing. What should he do? He began to despair. Like the marble that reflects the image, his face revealed his turbulent mind. The intelligent Gunabhushani then said, 'It's getting late. Let's discuss the rest tomorrow. If what I have said has made you unhappy, please forgive me....It's all for the good is the only consolation that I can offer.' The rest of the people left the room. Readers can decide for themselves what Kamalapuram Kantha's mental state was.

Kantha was scared. When she had hoped good things would happen, she had been struck by thunder. She left the place immediately and told her mother everything. Bhoga Chintamani's disappointment cannot be described They initially thought it was Mama's conspiracy but later changed their minds. Since there was no work left to do, they decided to return. Later, they decided to collect the remuneration for the concert and then leave. For Kantha's troupe, the day's events felt like a dream. They were astonished. It felt like Mama had added fuel to the fire.

Inauguration of the Conference: As announced in the newspapers, and in posters and pamphlets, the self-respect conference in Trichy started at 8 am. The entrance to the venue was decorated beautifully. Placards bearing slogans on social reform were placed side by side as if in a parade. Men and women thronged the venue. On the dais were Sornapuri zamindar, Dharmapuri zamindar, local dignitaries and officials. In the women's section, more than a hundred women were seated. When Gnanasundari, Gunabhushani and Sivaraman came to the dais, there was thunderous applause. Even after Mama and Somasekharan sent word several times, the Kamalapuram sisters were hesitant to come to the venue. Mama went in person and persuaded them to come.

The meeting began with two women singing self-respect songs. Gnanasundari proposed Gunabhushani's name as the Chairperson of the conference. She described Gunabhushani as follows:

'Sisters and Brothers, Elders, I think all of you know about Gunabhushani who will be the Chairperson of the conference. It's not an exaggeration to say that she is the beacon who has been born to help drowning women to cross the ocean of sorrow. Her work towards women's liberation has to be appreciated. This lady belongs to the devadasi community which is exalted by the scriptures and debased by society. Please forgive me for stating this openly. She realized the truth about the degradation of her community as well as how devadasi women create unending sorrows for the entire community of women. She has resolved to eradicate the system. Like a lotus blossoming in a stagnant pool, she was born in a depraved community but broke free of the shackles of dedication that bound the community and married a husband of her choice from another community and is now leading a meaningful life. He is her beloved husband. [She pointed to Sivaraman]. I don't have the skill or competence to describe the life of dedication to the cause of women suffering at the hands of wily devadasis. She is the personification of social reform. She is the walking angel who wipes the tears of virtuous women who have lost their husbands to the devadasis and lead the life of the living dead. She is the epitome of virtue as her name indicates. Hence, I humbly request her to accept the Chairpersonship of this conference.'

This proposal was accepted by the dignitaries and Gunabhushani chaired the session. Mama gave the welcome address:

'Dear sisters and brothers and respected zamindar. The points I want to highlight here are those that I was supposed to mention yesterday but I wanted to present them in front of both the zamindars. Some of the things might hurt some people. I may be questioned for carrying forward a ploy. However, to keep my conscience clear, I want to state all the things that I have done.

'My father was a wealthy man and I was his only son. So he was very indulgent. My name is Natarajan but no one calls me by that name. I am known as 'Minor' everywhere because I was forever spending lakhs and lakhs of rupees and practically lived in the houses of devadasis. There was a time when I didn't even think about my wife. At that time, I never thought in my dreams that my fortunes would change and I would be in this state. All my thoughts in those days were to surrender my wealth to the dasis and indulge in sensual pleasures. From that state to the present urge to do good to society happened mainly because of Gunabhushani Ammaiyar, the chair of the conference. I am happy to acknowledge it in public.

'In the thought that I can satiate the greed of the devadasis and experience heavenly bliss, I was travelling in first class by train to Chennai. At a station along the way, Kantha and Ganavathy boarded the train. I don't need to describe my thoughts on seeing them. Sensing that, these women thought that I was a fool (Laughter), I danced to their tune. Finally, they took away my ₹300 watch and citing their mother as the reason for not inviting me to their house, they alighted after giving me the wrong address.

Dear audience, listen further. I came to know later that they behaved this way because they thought that I was incapable. But at that time, I thought they were testing my affection and perseverance and not otherwise. Do we need any other example to describe my foolishness in adoring their pretentious words and deeds? By sheer good fortune, I reached Gunabhushani Ammaiyar's house. Initially I resisted her advice but later came to realize the narrow confines of naivete that had surrounded me. At that moment, I felt pure. Won't these women cheat other men as well? I decided to rout the entire group. I returned home after taking leave of Gunabhushani Ammaiyar. At home, the tug of war between my mother and my wife was fierce. Even at the risk of losing her son, my mother had informed my wife about my adventures with the dasis, with the sole aim of subduing my wife. When I saw this, I decided that parents are the cause for their sons going astray. After that, even though, I trod the path of domesticity, I couldn't forget how I lost my watch to Kantha and Ganavathi because I was gullible. I was waiting for an opportunity to teach them a lesson and also show the world a ray of hope. I received a wedding invitation from the zamindar seated here, Somasekharan. I attended the wedding. At that time, I understood Somasekharan's infatuation for Kantha and Ganavathi and how he was fast drowning. The groom Somasekharan got to know about me and sought my help to reach out to Kantha and her team and bring them into his fold. I refused but promised to send a pimp (Mama) and returned as Mama and took him to the house of Kantha (surprise and applause).

These women never asked him for anything explicitly. However covertly, they coaxed him to spend lavishly. When he spent two or three lakh rupees on jewellery, the elder zamindar forbade people from giving him loans. (Oho!) Then, these women completely ruined his life. I cannot describe the contrast between the treatment meted out to me in the train and the welcome accorded to me when I went as the Mama (loud laughter). There was no one to take care of the zamindar who had spent lakhs of rupees (laughter). Poor man, he was guarding the stairs. I collected a lot of information and to expose Somasekharan, I requested Gnanasundari Ammaiyar to don a disguise as a popular zamindar and took her to Kantha's house. Then I got hold of his signet ring and asked Somasekharan to take it to the elder zamindar and went to Kamalapuram.

When Gnanasundari was disguised as a zamindar, I found out that these women had total belief in tantra, astrology and witchcraft. Then, Gnanasundari and I returned to Trichy. I made her stay here and went to find out the condition of the younger zamindar, Somasekharan and his feelings for Kantha and others. I searched for him everywhere and found him under a tree. Even in that sinking state, he enquired after Kantha. I was not surprised because I have seen enough of people who are crazy about dasis. The zamindar and I decided to return to the zamin after curing him of this madness. I pacified him by requesting Gnanasundari to pose as dasi Kantha.

I disguised myself as a renowned tantric and performed pujas in Kantha's house to bring the new zamindar into their amorous fold. Gnanasundari didn't know about this. The rituals were performed with verve and vigour. They provided me with all the things I asked for. I employed many tricks and ploys to make them believe my sorcery. I made a letter arrive from the zamindar. I made money appear (laughter and applause). Listen to this joke. The place where the puja was performed was a dark room. Once, I stealthily brought a tortoise and placed a small head gear on it. It moved and when I lit the camphor, it stopped. Kantha and team believed that goddess Bhagavathy had descended and bestowed boons on them. Through these activities, I re-captured two lakh rupees worth of precious gems and jewels from them. Here are the jewels. (At this, Bhoga Chintamani fainted and the reason was obvious). I recovered the jewels that gullible men gave them but my watch has remained with them (laughter). I gave it up.

I realized that the recovered jewellery is not for my selfish purpose but to help the devadasi group to find a livelihood. When Kantha and group lost everything and were in a sorry state, I went to them again as a Mama. They assumed that I have brought a client. In an attempt to recapture their business, they gave me ₹2,000 to buy some artificial jewellery. I asked them to inform the police but they refused because it would affect their business. Please understand the shaky foundations of their existence. They have learned to cheat others and earn but do not know much abou worldly affairs. So, there is no surprise about what happens to them when they become old.

I took ₹2,000 from Kantha and group. I went back to bring them for this function. After I had taken the money and kept quiet, did they question me? No. Further, they went to the extent of claiming to be Gnanasundari, the zamindar's wife. So, I understood that if I showed them a way of earning money, I could use them in any manner. (applause). This speech stirred the entire audience.

3

Damayanti

In 1945, Moovalur Ramamirtham Ammaiyar wrote a story called 'Damayanti' in Dravida Nadu, *a magazine run by former Chief Minister CN Annadurai. This story was serialized for five weeks. One of the issues, dated 09.06.1945, is not traceable. It is difficult to say if this is because she did not write for a week or if that particular section has been lost. The parts that appeared in the four weeks seem to be in logical order. When we read the story as a whole, it does not look as if a week's worth of it is missing. The story has an easy flowing style. So, I believe that for whatever reason, the story did not appear in one issue.*

There is enough evidence that indicates that what we have is a fragment that was left out from the novel Dasigalin Mosa Valai. *Two characters—the head of the Mutt and Dharmapuri zamindar—appear in this story as well. She portrays how the head of the Mutt retains power and control and ensures that the devadasi system continue to exist. We can assume that the head of the Mutt in both the story and the novel is a real person, news about such a person was reported during the same period. Also, Thiru Vi Ka mentioned this person in his memoirs. Even though, 'Damayanti' is overtly propagandist, unlike* Dasigalin Mosa Valai, *it has been included here to reflect the present times.*

***

There are very few people who do not know about Bhuvanagiri zamindar, who ruled a fertile region. He had a daughter named Tamilarasi. There were two ministers—Venkatesa Iyer and Thirunavukkarasu—under his service. Since he ruled according to the scriptures, devotion to god, loyalty to Brahmins and belief in myths, legends and shastras were amply present in the zamindar. At the same time, his passion for Tamil was strong. It was very rare to find poets who had not won prizes in his court. There was no dearth for choultries, temples and mutts.

The zamindar appointed a learned head of the Mutt for the development of Tamil through schools to teach *Thevaram* and *Thiruvasagam*. He donated a large sum of money to the Mutt. He also engaged Madavadayal aka Manonmani dasi to do the work in the Mutt and Madanasundari dasi for temple work. The routine administration was carried out by Minister Thirunavukkarasu. In an administration focused on dharma, brahmins from different kingdoms were present. Like the free feeding for brahmins, the students of Thevaram School were given free food. One day, when the zamindar had a meeting of the council, his first minister informed him that dasi Madanasundari did not report regularly for temple work. The zamindar was furious and summoned Madanasundari.

King: Why don't you report regularly for temple work? Don't you know that it will reduce a part of divine hospitality? Won't the Lord get angry if the amorous offering is not done?

Madanasundari: O King! I was unwell. If I am unable to perform my duties, the Agama regulations permit the priests, their wives or brahmins to perform. How can you find fault with me alone? These rules have been made by the Brahmins. To avoid god's displeasure, can't they perform these duties?

King: Okay, you leave. Hmm.... If these thugs could perform according to tradition, why didn't they? Are the Mutt activities being performed regularly?

Thirunavukkarasu: I don't like the way the head of the Mutt functions. Unlike the brahmins who enjoy privileges (except for a few), the Tamil people are not treated well in terms of education, food....

King: [Calls the Head of the Mutt and asks] Why is there preferential treatment in teaching Thevaram and Thiruvasagam?

Head of the Mutt: It's the ordained law that only the pure can utter Thevaram and Thiruvasagam and not the untouchable shudra.

Thirunavukkarasu: We hired you to instil purity. Aren't you a Tamil person? So, the one who practises ritual purity is a noble shudra and the other is an ordinary shudra, is that right? Doesn't the ordained law pinpoint you as a distilled shudra and a concubine's son? Can't the Tamil speaking people chant the Thevaram? What's in that text that's unutterable by some? It only talks about the greatness of the temple pond and the fish in it. It's the attitude of people like you who chant scriptures to prevent the dissemination of this knowledge to all. Today, a Tamilian is considered inferior to a dog or a pig and is called the degraded shudra. Without understanding this reality, you insist on a sacred thread wearing shudra as the only one authorized to chant the Thevaram, like the belief that only brahmins can chant the Vedas. This just shows your ignorance in realizing yourself and I consider it a crime.

Head of the Mutt: You are the one who hasn't understood the difference. The ones who follow the traditions are equal to brahmins and wear the sacred thread.

Thirunavukkarasu: Excellent! If you are equal to brahmins, will they let you join them in a meal? While the brahmins consider you as a shudra, you create another marginal group? Please forget such thoughts and propagate the truth to the world. Don't all Tamil people make offerings and fall at the feet of the Sankaracharya? *The Laws of Manu* term a brahmin who doesn't chant the Vedas as a chandala. Do they at least fall at your feet? Even if one Tamilian thinks about it, would we lose our self-respect this way? If an enlightened person like you does not understand this, how will the illiterate do so? You were hired because we believed that education will lift the veil of ignorance and protect our self-respect. But if you start dividing people as superior and inferior, what's wrong in a brahmin criticizing us?

When he heard this passionate speech, the zamindar was furious and pronounced that Thirunavukkarasu has been removed from his post because he has insulted an elder. Deciding that serving the common people is better than working for an irrational king, he uttered the words, 'My pleasure' and left the place. The head of the Mutt happily reached the Mutt and the king went on to his place.

That night the king was distraught and sleepless about the fact that he didn't have a male progeny. 'If there's no male heir, how will I reach heaven? What if I am wealthy and perform virtuous deeds, if I am destined to reach hell.' He called for the priests to find out if there was a way to realize his goal.

***

'Giving birth to a male progeny is not easily achieved. Even though you haven't committed any sin in this birth, your sins in the previous births are the reasons for not begetting a boy. As a remedy, if you take a religious pilgrimage, a son will be born,' said the purohit.

The King said that given his advanced age, it was not possible to undertake the arduous pilgrimage and asked for some other way to propitiate the gods.

'All water bodies merge into the sea. All seas are confined in the feet of brahmins. So, donate generously to brahmins, wash their feet and drink the water. You will definitely beget a son.'

The King performed the stipulated rituals. But the birth of a son eluded him. He was heartbroken and made a plea to the head of the Mutt, who informed him that what had happened was ordained by fate. Realizing that there was no way of having a son, the King decided to make his daughter the heir and so employed a tutor named Damayanti to teach her. Since Damayanti had a radical bent of mind, she slowly instilled reformist ideas in the princess.

Thirunavukkarasu, who had been dismissed from the Minister's position, had started doing social work. He put forward his views and slowly started raising questions that interrogated the deeply embedded superstitions beliefs among people. Damayanti was dasi Manonmani's daughter. Manonmani understood the changes taking place in society and refused to dedicate her daughter. Instead, she gave her an education despite stiff opposition. Damayanti also studied well. She grew up into a beautiful young woman. On seeing this, her mother tried to force her into the traditional profession. Being an intelligent and competent woman, Damayanti refused to obey her mother. Madanasundari also informed her that the head of the Mutt had taken a fancy for her and that if she satisfied him, he would give a lot of money.

'What? Isn't he supposed to be an ascetic who has given up all forms of desire? Is he infatuated with me? No one would believe this,' said Damayanti.

'You don't know such things. It's a sacred doctrine.'

'Great! Good laws! They need to be incinerated. We need to eliminate the heinous act of forcing one community of women into prostitution. The god who created the world, who undertook the threefold acts of creation, protection and destruction, and the benevolent god, would he make someone his consort and make them public? Doesn't he have any shame? Further, there are many religions in our country and many castes. Those who are not brahmins are considered as shudras and untouchables. Why has our country degraded to this extent when noble men have been born here? Is the country which boasts of courageous men now filled with cowards? I am going to dedicate my life to help the women of our country lead a life of virtue, courage and strength. I have received help from the government to accomplish this task. You don't need to worry about me.'

When she heard these harsh words, Madanasundari returned home.

One day, the queen asked Damayanti about the real intentions of Thirunavukkarasu who was stirring the people up against the king. Damyanti said, 'Madam, in this kingdom, work done is not compensated appropriately. While people who do arduous work go hungry, some benefit from the hard work and lead an ostentatious life. So, the poor who face poverty and hunger hate the king. When there is no penury, no protests or revolutions can happen.' When she heard this, the queen promised that once she took over the rule, she would set things right.

Durairajan was the king of Dharmapuri, the mother of the whole of Tamil Nadu. He had reformist thoughts, broke the shackles of superstitions and provided good opportunities for people. His fame had spread far and wide. He had a son named Veera Gunaseelan. He was intelligent, knowledgeable, knew many languages and was well-versed in science. While the king was proud of his son's excellence in education, he was also concerned about finding a suitable bride who would match his virtuous character. He spoke to a friend about this concern. The friend suggested that Tamilarasi, who was the daughter of Gunasekara zamindar, the ruler of Bhuvanagiri, was also an educated and wise young woman and would be a suitable match for Veera Gunaseelan.

Durairajan thought about the matter. Bhuvanagiri zamindar was very wealthy and he was poor in comparison. Would he consent to this alliance? Deciding to take it forward, he sought the help of the priest Jayarama Iyer, who demanded ₹500 to forge the alliance. He went to Bhuvanagiri and informed his brother-in-law, Subbayyer, about this.

***

At that time, Tamilarasi had attained puberty. The king asked Subbayyer to study the horoscope. He drew some circles and mentioned some lagna and said that she would get married very soon. He said that the groom would come from the south and his name would begin with the letter 'V'. The king thought about it and decided that only Durairaja's son Veera Gunaseelan fitted that description. He wondered how this match was suitable, since Durairaja was not wealthy.

'Veera Gunaseelan! Yes, he's the one. The name starts with the letter 'V' as I had mentioned. No doubt at all. Things will happen as they are ordained. The horoscopes match well. She will be a Nitya Sumangali and not be widowed. She will beget a son. Don't hesitate. If you get her married to someone else, there would be a mangalya dosham leading to widowhood. Don't look at their wealth status. It's god's desire. 'Subasya Seekiram'—don't delay an auspicious occasion. Please arrange for the wedding immediately.'

The king also thought that destiny was playing out this way and sent his minister to Dharmapuri to finalize the alliance. The minister met Durairajan and convinced him and got his consent to arrange the engagement. He returned to Bhuvanagiri and told everyone about Veera Gunaseelan's intelligence, handsome appearance and compassionate nature and affirmed that he was the best suitor for Tamilarasi.

Meanwhile, Veera Gunaseelan came to know from his father about the alliance and wrote to Damayanti to find out her views and to ensure that the priest did not commit a mischief. He promised her that he wouldn't marry her, should the princess turn down the proposal. Damayanti was astonished on reading the letter and showed it to princess. On seeing his letter, the princess asked Damayanti to marry him.

'Don't be in a haste. There is a reason for mentioning both our names in the same letter. Since my community is known for being self-centered, he wants to know my views and at the same time, to test your affection. So, please don't take offence and send a suitable reply,' advised Damayanti.

The princess conveyed her acceptance. By that time, the king also confirmed that the alliance would go ahead as per the priest's guidance. Both the women were joyous about this happy turn of events.

Immediately, Damayanti informed Veera Gunaseelan about the acceptance of the princess. He was overjoyed on receiving the letter. In between, Durairajan went to Bhuvanagiri, asked the priest to suggest an auspicious date and arranged for the marriage to be conducted in a grand manner. Veera Gunaseelan and Tamilarasi led a happy life.

Veera Gunaseelan found a location in his kingdom where gold could be mined, obtained his father-in-law's consent and mined the gold. His father-in-law was very happy and proud about his son-in-law's intelligence, which increased his own wealth. As per the local custom, he donated one third of the gold to brahmins. Even though Veera Gunaseelan and Tamilarasi did not like it, they couldn't do anything.

When he heard this, Thirunavukkarasu went to the poor people and asked, 'Friends. You excavated the gold but the Aryans are reaping the benefit. What injustice is this? You don't get paid wages proportionate to your work. You get a pittance after doing strenuous work. Shouldn't this system be destroyed? Don't you have feelings? Don't you need encouragement?' Convinced by his passionate speech many people joined his outfit.

Some of the sanatana followers went and conducted discourses on the importance of dharma and pointed out how it is their duty to follow the tradition. But people refused to be swayed by their words. They went to the extent of preventing the meetings from being held. Yes! Truth triumphed.

One day, when Veera Gunaseelan was travelling in his car through a forest, the car was stopped and a cloth was thrown on the driver's head. An explosion was heard and subsequently, Veera Gunaseelan was not to be found. One man was found dead. The city was filled with cries and chaos. Telegrams and posts were despatched. Police investigated thoroughly. There was a notice announcing a reward of ₹10 lakhs to anyone who traced Veera Gunaseelan. But this was to no avail. On grounds of suspicion, the driver was arrested.

Two days later, a hunter brought the news that Veera Gunaseelan had been found dead in the forest. When the king and minister rushed there, they couldn't find his body but only his bloodstained clothes and ornaments. Everyone was convinced that he was dead. Following custom, the kind ordered the rituals to mark her widowhood and the princess was made to remove her wedding chain (thali) and wear the widow's garb of a white sari. Had it not been for Damayanti's support and consolation, Tamilarasi would have committed suicide.

***

One day, Thirunavukkarasu visited Damayanti in disguise and made a request. 'You need to bring out the driver who has been imprisoned by some means. I shall be forever grateful.' She consented and promised but requested someone who can act like a joker to help her.

The jail superintendent was more fond of dasi Manonmani than his own wife. He never parted from her and was always in her house. Damayanti met the superintendent's wife at an appropriate time and forged a strong friendship. One day, she went to the superintendent's house on a routine visit. That night without anyone's knowledge, she wore his clothes, made the joker dress up as the peon and went to the jail. She first inspected the sick unit and then went to the cell where the driver was confined. She made the driver wear the peon's clothes made the joker stay inside and escaped from the prison.

There was utter chaos and confusion inside the jail the next day. Police conducted an enquiry with the jail warden, who described what he knew. However, they couldn't elicit a proper response from the joker. Even though the government approached the situation from different angles, there was no clarity about anything. So, unthinkingly, the king tried to fix a reason for the disappearance of Veera Gunaseelan and the escape of the driver from the prison. He came to the conclusion that it was the unjust deed of an angry spirit. Sorcerers were summoned from within and outside the kingdom to exorcise the evil spirit. The towns were full of chaotic activities. The brahmins benefitted a lot from these. A lot of money was spent without any result.

Yet, the king was not pacified. Because his daughter was a widow, he assumed she was not fit to rule the kingdom and so handed over the administration to the minister. Will people who protested against the king, be submissive and accept the minister? There were protests, confusion and people were on the streets.

During this time, Damayanti and Tamilarasi conversed a lot. Damayanti suggested to Tamilarasi that they needed to work hard to erase the evils of the Hindu religion which has led to binaries and discrimination between men-women and ruler-ruled. Damayanti also decided to decimate the evil acts and deeds of the head of the Mutt. She wanted to visit the Mutt. She approached her mother and said to her that she deeply regretted going against her words. She promised to follow her advice from then on. The mother was happy and informed the head of the Mutt and left Damayanti in his care. At that time, he was advising his disciples about the need to overcome desire for land, women and wealth.

As soon as Damayanti entered, the disciples dispersed. Once they had gone, he started making amorous remarks. Damayanti interrupted him with many questions but he couldn't provide any apt responses. At that time, one of the disciples cleared his throat from an alcove. Immediately Damayanti trailed him without his knowledge. He embraced and kissed the woman who was waiting for him. Damayanti took a photo and returned to her original place. The head of the Mutt informed her that the young woman was the widowed daughter of Dhanakodi Chettiar, who had donated a lot of wealth to the Mutt. Damayanti asked him more questions. In the end, he informed her that it's difficult to control the natural urge and promised that he would never forget her.

Damayanti promised to return the next day, went directly to the princess, informed her about the nefarious activities and showed her the photo. The princess became furious. Damayanti advised her not to be furious and hasty. She asked her to keep it a secret, till the time was ripe.

Meanwhile, the king fell ill and died. Venkatesa Iyer came to Madavadaiyal's house and asked to speak to Damayanti. She was summoned immediately. Her mother left her alone. The minister informed her that since the princess does not have a progeny, she cannot rule the kingdom. However, he suggested a solution, that she can beget a child through a brahmin. He said the that Pandavas and Sankaracharya were all children of widows. He requested Damayanti to convince the princess and promised her a lot of money and valuables in return. Damayanti saw this as an opportune moment, promised to do the needful and she told the princess everything. The princess asked the minister if such an option existed. When he replied in the affirmative, she was furious and the minister left in a hurry.

Then the princess told Damayanti. 'I cannot put up with these atrocities any longer. I am going to rule the kingdom. Please inform the people and get their support.'

Damayanti informed Thirunavukkarasu about the decision of the princess. The very next day, he convened a big public meeting and made Damayanti chair the event. He clearly highlighted the virtues of the princess, the betrayal of the minister and the need for the princess to rule. Damayanti also spoke in detail after him. Social reformer friends like Rasayi Ammal made impassioned speeches. People decided that Tamilarasi should rule and offered to support her.

Many senior leaders were invited. Several rationalists, elders and prominent people accepted the invitation and attended. Suddenly, Veera Gunaseelan and Thirunavukkarasu arrived. People were overjoyed and raised slogans

'Long live Veera Gunaseelan! Long live Thirunavukkarasu!'

Based on the requests of people present there, Veera Gunaseelan and Tamilarasi remarried and Thirunavukkarasu and Damayanti had an inter-caste marriage. Thousands of poor people were fed and given clothes. The wishes and greetings received from different quarters were read out. There was no limit to the extent of joy experienced by the people.

Tamilarasi and Damayanti discussed many reformist thoughts. Then Thirunavukkarasu outlined his revolutionary deeds and the abduction of Veera Gunaseelan. He also hailed Veera Gunaseelan's contributions, who, in turn, eulogised Thirunavukkarasu's deeds.

Veera Gunaseelan and Tamilarasi enacted laws to eradicate superstitions, the atrocious activities of the heads of Mutts and the high handedness of the wealthy. They treated everyone equally. Thirunavukkarasu and Damayanti worked shoulder to shoulder with them.

Adhering to the new laws, the heads of Mutts apologized to the people and taught Tamil education effectively. For his heinous deeds, ex-minister Venkatesa Iyer was banished from the kingdom. The kingdom was filled with affection and scholarly activities increased.

4

Islam and the Status of Indians

Moovalur Ramamirtham Ammaiyar wrote and published this essay on 01.07.1939. It is being republished after 68 years. The publication assumes importance in the contemporary context of religious fundamentalism and the oppression of minorities. It is reproduced here in its entirety.

The word Islam means peace and conciliation. I decided to write about it because the Tamil ideology and Islamic ideology are similar. I didn't write this to convert but with an intention to present the travails of the Tamil people, who have always believed in the dictum 'All the universe is our place and everyone in this universe is our people,' One community, One God, and Love is God. Due to Aryan indoctrination, people have lost rational thinking, are enslaved and the demon of caste has taken hold.

People who believe in equality know that Comrade EV Ramasamy Periyar has instilled self-respect among the Tamils.

Haven't there been other such thinkers? We may ask. There were. One such was the noble soul born in Arabia 1400 years back, Thiru Nabhi Mohammad (Sal). He erased the worship of many gods–polytheism–and considered equality among faiths through Islam and we find Muslims leading a life of equality till today.

We may raise the question as to how the belief system reached India. It is surmised that some Arabians travelled to India. The indigenous tribal people who were not bound by the Aryan conspiracy may have embraced Islam. We find conversions till date.

Who can deny that people in the Aryan shackles hated and made a propaganda that it is impure to mingle with Muslims and to see them is a sin. In this way, they divided and ruled. Have they stopped the propaganda? Not at all. We find a conspiracy to break a true friendship in that EVR Periyar is projected as an atheist to the Muslims and as someone who strives to convert people to Islam among the Tamils. However, we find a synergy in the democratic spirit that nations strive for and what our country needs. These are reflected in the Self-Respect Movement as well.

'From whoever we hear a statement
it's important to decipher the truth in it.'

As these lines indicate, it's important to understand the true message of any religion instead of dividing and ruling.

Understanding the essence of Islam

1. There should be one caste and multiple castes should be done away with. Whichever caste is combined with Islam, it becomes one caste.
2. Untouchability: The one who is a paraiyan in the morning can convert into Ibrahim Sahib and visit a brahmin's house by evening.
3. Prohibition: The one who drinks to excess in the morning can be absolved by evening.

4. Equality: A pauper and a king can dine together.
5. Reduction of poverty: A rich man has to pay a tax of ₹2.80 for every ₹100.
6. Women's liberation: Access to property.
7. Brotherhood: If any one faces harm, everyone joins hands. Is this belief present in any religion?

Even though many like Buddha, Ramanuja and Christians were reformers, they have been influenced by the Aryan practice and casteism and polytheism exist.

Our Tamilians follow the ancestral practice of innumerable caste distinctions. I think we, who analyse many minute ideas, have not thought about this. If anyone scrutinises this idea and watches without any vengeance, they would set aside the superstitions beliefs and follow the path of equality. We can observe the western practice.

However, the Aryan belief and conspiracy has not been able to break the code of Nabi Nayagam (Sal). Why was it so? Since he didn't claim to be a reincarnation, and didn't scheme against kings and Gandhi could not set him aside.

We, who boast of the Tamil identity, are swayed by reincarnations. Since it's expected of us to follow the dictum, people have been led to believe men as divine avatars and have followed and still follow their scheming thoughts.

We give the plan of action ofThiru Nabi. Given the situation of the world at that point in history, there was a need for a superior ideology, which could show the way and a man who could lead and he was Nabi Gal (Sal).

This was what he preached. There will be no Nabi after me. I leave behind a plan for mankind, which encompasses the things required for human existence. My plan is not against nature, it will be acceptable to all people and beyond any doubts or discussion. I am responsible for my preaching. If you have any doubts, clarify them with me. Unlike the Aryan religion there is no reason to accept a dictum unconditionally.

We wish to place the following information for those who ask if self-respect ideology would work.

The situation in that country

The majees in Iran and Christians in Rome were world leaders. In India, there was a decline of Vedas, Ramayana, Mahabharata, Buddhist and Jaina dominance. The epic and puranic era in India began in 500 AD. People consider this the dark age. In this situation, Thiru Nabi (Sal) was born in April, 571 AD.

In Iran, people worshipped footwear and did many sinful deeds. The religious leader Maani preached for the need to destroy the world and abstain from marrying. He saw no other way to overcome the evil.

After him was born Mustaq. He preached the importance of making women, wealth and world as common property and leaving everyone free to act independently. At the time when Thiru Nabi attained the stature of a prophet, the Roman empire was in the last phase of decline. Fearing the enemies, all activities had been stopped in the Roman capital.

Sensual pleasures had reached their zenith. Prof. Gibbon, an eminent historian, states that there seemed to be no requirement of marriage.

Christianity was divided and war ensued. Two groups were competing for the post of bishop and there was a skirmish. Kings believed that it was not a sin to kill those who didn't conform to a religion.

The Indian situation

Kings were believed to be aspects of Brahma and incarnations of god. Lords and religious leaders were worshipped as gods. The affluent lords disrupted human morality and the religious leader made people irrational. All over the world, slavery was rampant and people were treated worse than animals. From the age of the Puranas till that of the Vedas, 33 gods were replaced by 33 crores of temples for gods and the so-called protectors became custodians of bad habits. (The devadasi system is a case in point.)

They worshipped man and woman in nudity. (Paundariga Yagam). Under the niyoga marriage, a widow can have a child by copulating with a brahmin. It was not permitted with other castes. In the name of god, women were forced into prostitution and it was sanctioned as divine duty. Salvation was promised for those who drank cow's urine. If an untouchable even touched an upper class woman, he was sentenced to death. If he read the Vedas, his tongue was severed. Any shudra who dared to covet a brahmin's belonging was tortured. But, a brahmin could covet a shudra's belongings. If a shudra had a relationship with a brahmin girl, his private parts would be severed and his body was butchered. However, a brahmin could copulate with any woman. We can find similar atrocities sanctioned in the *Laws of Manu.*

Likewise, in Arabia also, the situation was completely degraded. Everywhere there was idol worship, heinous acts and murder of girls. People took many wives. When they had to eat meat, they would eat the choicest parts from live animals. When there was drought, they would tie hay on the tail of a cow and burn it. In that Arabian desert was born Thiru Nabi.

Nabigal's aim was to create a plan for human life and any man who followed the code was considered to be human.

Even when fathers and forefathers had broken the code, he emphasized that the duty of man was to obey the truthful laws. When laws are true, they don't change. Only through this, can men become civilized.

The belief in god is the human belief in a natural power. Due to negligence and forgetfulness, people lose this power and sometimes face a generational lapse. The Quran preaches higher thinking in a heart bereft of joy and enthusiasm.

The belief of Christianity is that men are born sinners. Hindus believed that men are born with a destiny that is the result of sins in the past births. What Nabi preached was as follows:

'Man's nature is good. It seeks goodness and hates evil. So, if an individual seeks to achieve a sublime level, nature will aid.'

This echoes the belief of Tamils that of all the births, the human form is the rarest.

What is to be performed in action is the outcome of the thought and belief of an individual. Thoughts lead to actions. Our Periyar also states the same idea. Is it wrong?

So, if thoughts are purified, their life is pure and reformed. In order to rein in the idea, Nabigal insisted on a five-fold path called Imaan.

The Five-fold Path

1. There is one creator who created you and others. He is compassionate but punishes the sinner harshly.
   Note: In other religions, there is the concept of redemption from sins. If there is no way of redemption, will anyone dare to commit a sin? Only because of the belief in redemption people dare to perform offerings, pilgrimages, offer cows to the priests and believe that they can cross purgatory to

reach heaven. Or they seek forgiveness from the religious leaders by offering material gifts. The law that there is no redemption for sins is a lofty thought.

2. People who know that there are things beyond comprehension and beyond the physical world, do not commit sin and obey the divine laws. Through this belief, he understands the truth.
3. In every community there are good people who are truthful and preach the same idea. We need to confirm that there is no need for divisions and subsects. The purpose is to consider everyone as brethren.
4. We need to accept all the scriptures bestowed on Nabi by Allah. Instead of divisionary tactics, we need to accept truth wherever it is present.

Just as god is common to all, shouldn't religions also be common? The purpose of religions is to regulate and not divide into groups and fight. Self-centred people may interpret ideas to suit their own needs. The fourth way has been established to desist this.

EVR Periyar emphasizes this idea when he calls for removing the profanity in Hinduism. Is it justified to term him an atheist?

5. Following the deeds in this earthly sojourn, after death, a new world will provide happiness. The new world is a haven of peace.

All these five dictates are called Imaan in Islam. They were put forth to bring about good thoughts.

Just as the loyalty oath in kingdoms not to misuse the power vested by authority, Thiru Nabi's spiritual governance demanded people who wanted to join Islam to take the oath that they would adhere to the life principles enshrined by Allah and that there is nothing equal to Allah. Thiru. Nabi is the messenger. These two oaths were considered important.

The Imaan offered five times every day is announced in the Muezzin's call to come to the mosque. Those who attend should ensure cleanliness and hygiene. During the hour of prayer, everyone needs to obey the one law and believe that there is no difference between rich and the poor. At this time there will be a discourse on unity, a merger with the divine, and social reform.

Besides, on two days in a year, all Muslims of a particular area would offer prayers in a large ground. This is known as the prayer of the Big Day. This community worship is considered the best way to bring people together. It offers the advantage of providing an opportunity to talk to others.

At present, it is difficult to convene a large public meeting to spread useful messages. Even if such a meeting is convened, its effect will be short lived. However, by making community meeting and discourse part of the norms of worship, it is not easily erased.

Jakkaat is a tax paid once a year out of the profit made in business dealings with silver, gold, land, houses and agricultural produce. ₹2.80 is paid for every ₹100. The tax that is collected is used to support people who are unable to find livelihoods, the infirm, sick, orphans, widows, travellers, students and loan defaulters. Because of this, the poor and rich feel compassionate towards each other. Instead of making it an individual act of kindness, it is offered as a community support maintained by public funds. This curtails any sense of arrogance felt by the benefactor or the feeling of shame and embarrassment felt by the beneficiaries.

If people feel it is important to have a just government, this plan ensures that the powerful and wealthy are not hated by the poor. Will the poor suffer? Will people protest against the taxes imposed by the king? Our conclusion is that Nabi Gal's norms are better than the socialism propounded by Russia, where there is dictatorship. If the authorities or people disagree, the ideology would fade away. The Islamic law would survive till the last Muslim stands.

To erase the difference between the poor and rich, for one month in a year, fasting is observed. The idea is to experience hunger and provide a break from eating and drinking. During this time, it is also important to refrain from evil thoughts, telling lies, gossip, using derogatory words and indulging in immoral activities. By the end of the fasting period, this becomes a habit. Usually associations celebrate founder's day but Nabi Gal has made it a religious dictum and not as a socio-cultural practice. So, no one can change it. Also, the fast becomes a way of cleansing the system arising out of the negligence of the body. Evil habits such as drugs and addiction are overcome. People get used to living a simple life. Further, the rich understand the pangs of hunger felt by the poor. A sense of equality prevails. Lethargy is reduced and patience, philanthropic thoughts and tolerance are enhanced.

Aim of Haj

There is one creator. Even though we are divided in terms of religions and nations, we are identified as human beings. We need to come to the unanimous decision to follow the laws propounded by the protector of the world. Everyone needs to wear the same kind of clothes. They need to shave at the same place. Even small creatures like mosquitoes and flies should not be harmed. People who feel Islam is not compassionate need to make a note of this. When performing the Haj, people come together with a firm belief that all are humans. This leads us to the path of oneness in nature.

EVR explains this idea by stating that individuals should cultivate the sense of human kind and strive for self-respect. Even Nabi Gal does not call himself a Mahatma. Even Periyar never claims that.

Let us now consider in brief the virtue, morals, discipline and life of unity propounded by Islam. We have already explained the context of Nabi's teachings. He has prescribed laws to enable man to reach his supreme natural potential.

A true Muslim cannot be a coward or weak but should be compassionate and courageous without ego. He should view courage as a life skill but should not be a problem maker. He should be happy and content with what he has but should not stop persevering. He should respond to the call of peace but not back out, should there be a need to fight a war. He should be educated but without self-importance. He should be a believer. He should not debase his body. He should be pure at heart and not have wicked thoughts. In all matters, he should differentiate between good and evil.

However, he should bear with any suffering arising accidentally. He should be compassionate even towards his enemies but should uphold justice without consideration for friends and relatives. While talking to the poor, he should talk politely and raise them. He should respect conviction, self-belief and conscience. However, he should not get fooled by giving money to one who doesn't deserve it. He should be friendly but keep troublemakers at a distance. Even though he should not mistrust anyone, he should be cautious. He should not boast about his deeds of charity. He should treat the whole world as his kin but should follow the divine laws of creation. He should work and respect elders but should not become a renunciate. He should lead the life of a householder without getting enslaved by it. He should follow religious dictates without losing sight of rationality.

We can question if Thirukkural does not propound these virtues. Even if it is contained in the Kural it is not practised and that is why Periyar preaches it. Is it fair to label him as atheist?

Intellectuals criticise EVR as someone not highly educated. It is only to prove that there is no connection between education and rationality that I have cited the example of Thiru Nabi (Sal). Those who possess bookish knowledge, let them give respect to the path shown by the illiterates. Nabi Gal was not educated and didn't have the opportunity to learn from the wise till his enlightenment. Despite this, he was a teacher for the world.

Till today, people of many nationalities and religions like his template for democratic rule. However, in those days, archery, singing eulogies and understanding the historical lineage were the most important requirement for the Arabians. People who didn't follow these, were not respected in that country. Nabi Gal Nayagam neither learnt this art nor was he interested in it. By and large he was silent and didn't indulge in useless activities. When he expressed his views on a matter, they would be the best and reveal his intelligence. His discipline enabled him to live along with his enemy, friend, stranger, kin, poor and rich while also being detached.

Among Arabians, fasting meant to stay awake and pray. Thiru Nabi told them that they are responsible for their body, eyes and wife. So, it is better to fast three times in a month but they didn't agree.

The sahibs believed that Nabi Gal would also follow the practice of incessant prayers but found him to be devoid of sin. While one decided to pray through the night, the other wanted to fast throughout his life and the third decided not to marry. Nabi Gal advised them as follows:

'I state this in the name of God. Listen, fear and follow God more than you. I fast and sometimes I don't. I live with my wife and children. Those who don't follow my path do not belong to my community.'

It seems as though Nabi Gal was a homely ascetic. Let us describe in brief his domestic life. Till the age of 50, he lived with one wife. After her death, for various reasons, he took many wives. He was just to all of them. He distributed food equally and would visit all the houses and take care of their needs. He would take turns to spend the night.

If he had to travel, he would choose the one to accompany him through lots. As he grew old and infirm, he still stayed by turns. Even when he was not mobile he would take help. On realizing his sufferings, they unanimously permitted him to stay with one wife.

He preached what he practised. Those who are good to the family are good. If a man is displeased with his wife, he should keep her away from the bed chamber. Neither should he leave the house nor should he turn her out of the house. He cautioned people about how excessive praise will spoil a person. We find him to have lived a life of the Mahatma and instil that sense in a religion.

Freedom for Women

1. Property rights: One third of the father's property and meher of 166-4-0 was to be given by the husband.
2. If a man divorces his wife, he has to pay 166-4-0. Women didn't need to divorce.

3. Widow remarriage: For four and a half months after the husband's death, the wife is to be protected by a female guardian. If she is pregnant, after her delivery and with her assent, she can be married. The child can remain with her or with the husband's family. It is the duty of the husband's family to take care of the mother, child and wife. The child will have rights to the property of his/her biological father
4. A man who is capable of satisfying them can take two wives. Even if one is rich and the other is poor, he has to treat them equally and with affection.
5. If a woman indulges in prostitution, it has to be proven with a witness. We may question how it is possible. In Islam, male prostitution is also censured. Is it not a lofty thought that an unproved mistake is not considered a sin?
6. Education is common for all, unlike The *Laws of Manu* which forbade women's education

Plans for Democratic Rule

In Nabi Gal's reign, the tax was paid in gold.

Good Deeds for Non-Muslims

1. It is not mandatory to do military service
2. If enemies attack, Muslims should protect and support non-Muslims
3. They should not be forcibly converted
4. It is a Muslim's duty to protect the life and property of others
5. Their jobs and representation cannot be removed or taken away
6. No place of worship of other religions should be considered inferior and destroyed

7. One-tenth of the tax paid by the Muslims should be levied from others
8. Their property should not be confiscated. No Muslim should force others to turn away from their faith

Would not such a rule be peaceful? Think about it. Will Muslims accept the present form of democracy?

We are stating these only to prop up the Tamilians. Nabi Gal, who conceived such a lofty ideal, had to leave his country owing to the atrocities of the Mecca Kureishis and Jews. Weren't his teachings the path of truth?

In Arabia, Mushrikins were the dominant community. They followed idol worship and accepted Allah as the God but believed that other gods also existed. They thought that natural occurrences, good and evil were the results of heavenly objects. They would seek permission from these heavenly bodies before commencing any work. Their hearts were deeply given to the idol worship.

To erase this belief was considered the foremost duty, the Quran Sharif does not highlight this aspect but emphasizes the need to overcome this belief in verses 27, 61, 62, 63 and 64. We are not presenting the sufferings caused by this. In Abyssinia and other nations, Muslims were divided. They spread the message wherever they travelled. It was contested by Jews, Christians and Mushrikins.

144 people who went to the discourse in Arabia were killed. So, it became important for them to carry weapons. Dissenters interpreted it as forced conversion. Should truth be enriched by brute force? Did the self-respect ideas spread so extensively because of brute force?

Hence, it is important to discern from our readings of Sal's path what is to be included and discarded. It is certain that if they practise discernment, they will reach a level free of any blemish. Tamil people who are knowledgeable and those who belong to tribal communities will accept this. The country should be well and devoid of Aryan domination. Tamil Nadu for Tamilians—the feeling should prevail.

Glory be to Nabi Gal Nayagam (Sal)!

Felicitations to Periyar!
Written by Moovalur Ramamirtham Ammaiyar

5

Other Writings

Moovalur Ramamirtham Ammaiyar wrote the novel Dasigalin Mosa Valai *or* Mathi Petra Minor, *she serialized the story 'Damayanti' and a short work 'Islam and the Status of Indians'. She also wrote essays from time to time. It was our good fortune that some handwritten manuscripts (which were fragile and crumbling) of unpublished essays, were with her family. That collection consisted of one article on Pavendar Bharathidasan, another on the status of women and the third comprised a few pages of her passionate work on her women's association activities in the 1940s. These essays exemplify Ammaiyar's vast knowledge and her open views and uninhibited opinions on different areas such as language, arts, culture, women's status, education, development and politics. Some of them have been included here.*

1. Met the Mother

It was nearly one o'clock at night. I could not sleep. I decided to spend some time on the Cauvery river front, and went and sat on a sand heap. It was a full moon night in the month of Chithirai. The moon was white like milk. It was pleasantly cool.

The gentle breeze of spring brought with it a pleasant fragrance of flowers which made me happy. I spread my towel and lay down and fell into a gentle sleep.

When I woke up, I found someone sitting a little distance away and crying. I listened carefully and it was definitely the sound of crying. Who could it be at this time of the night? I was scared that it was a ghost. Gathering courage, I decided to go and find out. I inched closer.

'Who are you? Why are you sitting on the river bank in the dead of the night and crying?'

There was no reply. Nor did the crying stop. I was convinced that it was some kind of evil spirit. Hardening my stance, I asked rather firmly, 'Are you going to tell me who you are or not?'

'Son, don't you know me?'

'If I knew, would I ask?'

"Am I not your mother?'

I was shocked.

'Why should my mother come from Kumbakonam to the sand banks of the Cauvery?'

As I continued in this vein, she asked,

'Oh Son, am I not your Tamil mother?'

I observed her closely. The flavour of Tamil wafted from her. Realizing that she was indeed the Tamil mother, I prostrated myself at her feet.

'Please forgive me mother,' I said.

She blessed me.

'Mother, why are you crying? Please tell me what is wrong.'

'Son, what's the use of telling you? You are a carefree youth. You study in the college and eat food at the hostel comfortably. You are a person who spends life without understanding the state of your mother. Not only you, but many of my Tamil children are like that. First things first, you must realize that the alien Aryans are troubling me.

'Mother, I don't understand your words. Please explain. Thus far, I have neglected my duty towards my mother tongue, in my ignorance.'

'Listen to me carefully, son. I'll tell you. First, let's take the Tamil used in magazines and newspapers. Is it even Tamil, I ask? They have butchered me by mixing the words of the Aryan language. They call it spoken Tamil. It is the transliteration of the brahmanical slang into Tamil letters. My own people buy, read and enjoy the newspapers which degrade me. They don't notice my yearning. Even though they have the sixth sense, in their ignorance they become foolish and feel happy. A true Tamil son should not even touch those magazines. Can you do that?'

Her words were sharp and forceful.

'I'll do it, Mother. From today, that will be my oath.'

'Secondly, take music. Terming them as Tamil lyrics, they torture me. Let them sing in Telugu. This is my request. Can they just translate lyrics from northern languages and call them Tamil songs? People enjoy these as well and claim to enjoy the music.'

'Do you think that their enjoyment is real? Can it be due to ignorance?' I interrupted. 'No, no, I think they do it knowingly. Some may do it out of ignorance but….'

'Let me tell you about the dialogues and songs in theatre and movies. All of them use brahmanical Tamil. It is not really our language, Son.'

'Yes, Mother. Since I watch Tamil movies regularly, I have noticed.'

'Son, there is no point in blaming the enemies. I am grieving at the naivete of my people. I will not stay here anymore. I will go somewhere else. I have decided that it is better to put a veil over my head rather than meet the people who have forgotten their mother. Without my knowledge, I have shed tears in the central Kudanthai region of the Cauvery delta. I should go.'

She got up to leave.

'Mother, I plead with you. Don't go.'

I held her feet and pleaded with her.

'No, I think it's better I leave. Let me tell you something else. The Tamil region was not formed yesterday. It was formed millions of years ago. The Tamil Nadu of yore extended from the Vindhyas in the north to the Indian ocean in the south. From Java islands in the east, it extended to Madagascar in the west. Over time, the territory has been subsumed by the sea and the region today has shrunk. Many of my dear people were born and died as poets. Valluvan! Ilango! I have lost them. Today, I have but one son. He is my beloved son. Without him, Tamilians would have sunk into a bottomless pit. Had he not been born, I would have vanished without a trace. The Aryan visitors who came would have vanquished me.'

'Who is this precious son, my mother?'

'Do you know Puducherry?'

'Yes.'

'The one who has assumed the name Bharathidasan—Kanaga Subburathinam—is my beloved son.'

'Oh Yes! I know him and his works, Mother. He is a revolutionary poet.'

'It's because of that revolutionary poet that people still survive. But even though all Tamils are my own, they are ungrateful. Bereft of emotions, they are humans who do not have Tamil blood in their veins.'

She spoke with so much anger and emotion. 'Please don't get angry, Mother.'

'I know that they have neglected me but they have also neglected him. They lack the brains to understand his poems. Swayed by the brahmanical propaganda and associating with them…'

'They are ready to fight with fury. Our work is to vanquish the enemies and to develop Tamil. We will not let down our poet. We respect him a lot. You don't need to go anywhere, Mother.'

I held on to her feet.

'Son, I appreciate your love for Tamil language. Because you are requesting me to stay, I will do that. Do your duty towards the mother. Victory will be yours.'

2. The Status of Women in our Country

Dear Mothers! I am going to speak my views on the status of women in our country. Think. That our country was developed in terms of domestic bliss than any other country is understood by all thinking people. However, scholarly and intellectually superior, no one refrained from marriage. The reason is that a spouse is the best companion who supports the forsaken, the poor and the dead, following Thiruvalluvar's dictum. In the domestic sphere, women (more than men) assumed responsibility for running the household. Women led their lives with natural intelligence even though they were not educated, as was evident in their restricting the expenditure within the husband's income, bringing up the children, putting up with wayward husbands, bearing the torture of mothers-in-law and sisters-in-law, welcoming the guests and anticipating the arrival of guests.

Currently, women have not understood the domestic life of our women of the past. They have adopted an ostentatious life and spend more than their husbands' earnings. Instead of guarding the family structure, they have started breaking it. Like the proverbial truth that women can create or destroy things. Like the mixing of cowdung in a delicate perfume, our women have been degraded. Why? The poor and simple women have started following the ostentatious standard of living of rich women. Did they benefit? They only saw themselves in the grip of evil.

In early times, mothers would teach their daughters respectful behaviour, thrifty planning through combined cooking (*kootanchoru)*, how to strengthen the body through household chores and games like *sobanam kottal, kolattam, thumbi sutral, nila poochi,* hide and seek and many others. While bringing up boys, they would emphasise the different ways of interpersonal interactions and the importance of education.

Besides these, every woman was familiar with home remedies. Unlike now, when people rush to the doctor or the traditional healer for every small ailment, every household had stored knowledge equal to that found in universities. Some say that times have changed and values have been forgotten. It is not time which has changed. Have day and night been interchanged? Or vice versa? Has our nation migrated elsewhere? Are humans giving birth to beasts and vice versa? None of these have changed. Practices of yore will not change.

O Mothers! Look at your daughters. Because they lack physical strength, they look frail, hunched and devoid of feminine beauty. Besides, without realizing that unplanned childbirths happen due to lack of physical strength, women search for contraceptive methods. If our nation has to develop, following ancient practices, both educated and uneducated women have to bring up their daughters with natural bodily strength and without any ostentation. Did women in the past not lead happy lives with their natural beauty? Did they seek artificial methods to enhance their beauty, by applying layer after layer of cuticura powder on their faces, wearing danglers that touch their shoulders, wearing excessive jewellery and expensive clothes? Spending beyond their means, they buy blouse pieces of three yards by borrowing. If the poor buy three yards, won't the rich woman spend on 30 yards? Do you think people would underestimate us if we didn't follow these ostentatious practices?

If you take 10 well-dressed women out for a stroll, others will try to imitate their style. This is the nature of women. From where did these unknown beauty practices come? Did they emerge out of a resolution in a women's conference? They emerged from imitating one another. There is also a new fashion of wearing blouses, saris and accessories like bangles, earrings and flowers in the same colour. Will they paint themselves black if they wear black clothes? It would be more justified to paint their faces red, green and yellow to match the clothes. Don't get me wrong. Our country has degraded because we have committed the sin of encouraging excessive expenditure. Is there a reason for famine in our country? Can a land which mined gold face such deprivation? In earlier times, did our women have to face this kind of situation? During times when there were no Marwaris or banks, women lent money. Their honesty cannot be matched by banks. Men may face a cash crunch but not women. Poor women would save money by making and selling cow dung cakes. Women had practised micro-finance methods through *siruvadu*. These days women spend. Mothers! It is high time we realize our mistakes. Rich women need to think carefully. Our country should prosper. I would like to conclude by recalling that a woman can make or mar the world. Vanakkam.

3. Women's Education

Education is very important and necessary for women to progress well at the familial and national levels.

Education will show the right path –
A man may not know till he is educated.
A woman will learn without books
To show the path of goodness.

Like for men, education is very important for women. Women bear a greater responsibility in running the family.

Women need education to run the family in the right way and manage the finances. In foreign countries, women have proved themselves in many fields. The reason is that men and women have been treated as equals and been provided education.

In countries like America and Russia, women have invented many things. They have done research in technology and science. Those countries have developed and garnered praise from many intellectuals. These feats have been made possible by education.

Since we treat men and women differently, women's education is perceived very differently. Some parents are against education for women. Perhaps this is because women are mainly trained to take on domestic work or because there is the custom of preventing girls from going outside the home after puberty or because parents are suspicious.

For women to know about hygiene, to take care of children and to run the family in a healthy manner, from childhood till they are married, they are trained by the affectionate advice of the mother. Hence it becomes the duty of the woman of the house. Then, isn't education important for them?

In foreign countries, 90 out of 100 women are educated. But in our country even 10 out of 100 girls are not educated. In foreign countries, proper arrangements have been made for educating girls. In our country, even at present when equality for women is demanded, such arrangements have not been made. Women do not have the right to be educated. This is very unfortunate. The evil fate of our nation is our parents. Foreign countries have developed in all spheres due to education. Can there be any reason other than lack of education for the degradation of our country? Will parents and the government take steps in this direction?

4. On behalf of Mayavaram Women's Welfare Association*

12 February, 1944

A group of people met at Comrade Moovalurar's house and unanimously decided as follows:

1. The aims of the Association are women's development, education, and thrifty maintenance of the family;
2. The annual subscription fee for members is 4 annas;
3. If other leaders are invited, a fee will be collected according to expenses incurred;
4. The secretary will maintain the income and expenditure register;
5. The funds collected cannot be spent without the approval of the committee;

---

* Mayavaram Women's Welfare Association was a women's association. They had their monthly meetings even during the world war. They did not discuss domestic issues but actively debated social and political matters. These minutes of meeting portray their activities.

6. After the 25th of every month, there will be a discourse in Moovalurar's house.

Ramamirtham Ammaiyar, Vaduga Street.

On behalf of Mayavaram Women's Welfare Association

24.03.1944

At 4 pm, 50 women met at Moovalurar's house. She spoke on women's development and thrifty measures to be adopted during times of war. Secretary Pankajathammal proposed a vote of thanks and the meeting ended.

24.04.1944

At 3 pm, under the leadership of Moovalurar, a meeting was held at C Raja Padmavathy Ammal's house. Issues related to women's development and education were discussed. Secretary Mangalathammal proposed a vote of thanks and the meeting ended.

25.06.1944

Many women assembled at 4 pm in Raja Padmavathy Ammal's house under the leadership of Moovalurar. Thanjavur Glory Moses spoke on 'Women's Duty during War.' After the chairperson offered the concluding remarks and S Raja Padmavathy Amma thanked everyone, the meeting ended.

25.07.1944

At 5 pm, a meeting was held under the leadership of C Raja Padmavathy. Many women participated. Glory Moses talked about 'War and Thrifty Practices by Women.' After the chair gave closing remarks, K Pankajam thanked everyone and the meeting ended.

25.09.1944

At 4 pm, there was a public meeting at Siddarkadu Vaduga Street. Many women had gathered under the leadership of Moovalurar. She spoke on 'The Domestic Life of Ancient Women'. After she highlighted the need to avoid unnecessary expenses and superstitions, C. Raja Padmavathy Ammal proposed the vote of thanks and the crowd dispersed.

20.11.1944

The meeting took place at 5 pm in C Raja Padmavathy Ammal's house under the leadership of Moovalurar. After many spoke on women's responsibilities during war time, S Mangalathammal thanked everyone and meeting ended.

20.12.1944

At 4 pm, in Siddarkadu Vaduga Street in C Raja Padmavathy Ammal's house, women met under the leadership of Moovalurar. Many women spoke on how to manage expenses during the times of war. After the concluding remarks, the secretary thanked everyone and the meeting concluded.

15.01.1945

A meeting was held at 4 pm in Siddarkadu Vaduga Street house of C Raja Padmavathy Ammal and Moovalurar was the chair. Women talked about the rations received during war and small savings. After the concluding remarks, the assistant secretary proposed a vote of thanks and the meeting ended.

22.02.1945

A women's meeting was held at 5 pm in the house of C Raja Padmavathy Ammal and it was chaired by A Ramamirtham Ammaiyar. The meeting addressed the importance of small savings during the time of war. C Raja Padmavathy concluded the meeting with a vote of thanks.

20.04.1945
A meeting of women was held at 4 pm in Siddarkadu Vaduga Street in the house of C Raja Padmavathy Ammal and was chaired by Moovalurar. The importance of thrift and small savings were discussed and concluding remarks were provided. K Pankajam Ammal proposed the vote of thanks.

No date
The following resolutions were unanimously passed between S Kumudavalli Ammal, Rajakantham Ammal, P Rajammal, Thayaru Ammal and Seetha Ammal.

1. Aims of the association: To conduct monthly meetings and discuss about ancient Siddha Vaidya practices;
2. To preach about women's health and hygiene through door to door campaigns;
3. To enlist women members;
4. To raise funds from time to time based on anticipated expenditure;
5. Location of the association's office: House of C Raja Padmavathy Ammal, Vaduga Street, Siddarkadu.

S Mangalathammal thanked everyone and the meeting concluded well.

11.08.1945
A women's meeting was held at 3 pm in the residence of C Raja Padmavathy Ammal under the leadership of Moovalurar. Many spoke on child development and Siddha practices to be

followed by women. After concluding remarks, the secretary proposed a vote of thanks and the meeting ended.

11.11.1945
A meeting was held at 5 pm in the SV Street residence of C Raja Padmavathy Ammal under the leadership of Moovalurar. Women's hygiene and education were discussed. The meeting concluded with a vote of thanks by the secretary.

19.12.1945
A public meeting was held at SV Street under the leadership of Moovalurar on behalf of the Mayavaram Tamil Siddha Vaidya Women's Association. A lot of women had gathered. After the opening remarks, C Vimala and S Savithri spoke on the need to show mercy. In that meeting, the resolution given below was unanimously passed.

This meeting requests the Hon'ble Governor of Madras to show mercy on MKThyagaraja Bhagavathar and NS Krishnan who were well-known film actors and who have contributed extensively to the war fund.

S Mangalathammal proposed K Pankajathammal seconded and the motion was passed unanimously. After the concluding remarks, C Raja Padmavathy Ammal proposed a vote of thanks. The petition was sent to the Hon'ble Governor of Madras.

Abolition of Devadasi System Act

Moovalur Ammaiyar worked extensively at the grassroot level to abolish the devadasi system. She received support from many progressive people. This protest concluded with the passing of Madras Devadasis (Prevention of Dedication) Act. The Bill was introduced in the Madras Legislative Council by Dr Muthulakshmi Reddy. Overcoming many obstacles, she was the first lady doctor in Tamil Nadu. She was the first Indian woman to be elected to the Legislative Council. She struggled hard to enact laws like the Child Marriage Restraint Act and Prevention of Polygamy under Hindu Marriage Act. Similarly, she took great pains to pass the bill on the abolition of the devadasi system. That is a separate history. In her autobiography in English, Muthulakshmi Reddy has written in detail about her struggles, the resistance she faced while introducing the devadasi Act and how she tackled the many issues that came up. She writes,

> For a long time, I was of the view that the devadasi system, which is continued in the name of religion, is an unjust practice and a violation of human rights. I thought that the practice was deeply rooted in society and the women were forced to live a life of degradation. Because of this, their physical and mental health was affected. I felt that it was against the higher ideals of our culture. So, I proposed a resolution to abolish this heinous practice and waited for

the country of votes. Luck favoured me. This resolution was passed and on 4th November and was listed in the gazette under my name. As usual, the conservatives opposed it strongly. They tried their best and spent their energy to reject the resolution. But I was firm. I took a vow to continue my fight till this shameful practice was abolished from the face of the earth.

When the resolution came up for discussion, as the proposer, I made a long speech emphasising the need to abolish the system. The Council welcomed my speech with applause. All the parties conveyed their support to my resolution. This speech was printed in Tamil and English and distributed.

Congress leaders like KR Karanth, CV Venkatramana Iyengar, Muthuranga Mudaliar, Anjaneyulu, Ministers AP Shetty, Syed Ibrahim, V Munusamy Pillai, SN Durai Raja and Deputy Leader of the Justice Party, Krishnan Nair, extended their wholehearted support to the resolution and spoke on it. At the same time, the then Law Minister CP Ramaswamy Iyer, while appreciating the importance of the resolution, also pointed out the problems that could arise in its implementation.

Later, some minor corrections were made and the resolution was passed unanimously. 'Since young girls or women are dedicated to Hindu temples, they are pushed into an immoral life. In an attempt to stop this practice, the government has to bring out a new Act; if the government is of the opinion that there may be some practical problems in implementation, then it can recommend to the central government to formulate a clear law. This is the recommendation of this Council.'

However, the local government forwarded the resolution to the central government without taking any steps to resolve the problem. So, I sought the help of a Legal Committee Member and developed a legal proforma to abolish the devadasi system, obtained approval from the Indian government and introduced it in the state assembly the next year.

After this, I was forced to tackle unique problems. While my contributions to education and medicine received extraordinary support, there was a refusal to recognize my social work. Those who didn't have the courage to criticise my social reform thoughts, covertly started working against me. They started two associations under false names and protested against the bill becoming a law and sent complaint petitions to the government. They also started false propaganda among the common people.

So, I had to spend all my energy to contest this false campaign. I wrote many articles in magazines to support my bill. I also wrote and distributed pamphlets among the common population. I garnered support for the cause of organizing several meeings for women. My efforts reaped their reward. Many groups openly supported the cause of abolishing the devadasi system. In many places, people organized meetings on their own and forwarded their resolutions to stop the dedication of women. Further, they openly opposed those who supported the devadasi system. Both Tamil and English magazines came forward to publish editorials and essays on the need to abolish the devadasi system. In particular, many women from the devadasi community broke away from the system in many places. They also passed resolutions to eradicate this heinous practice completely. So, I obtained their support. Through this, my struggle received more impetus and conviction!

Prohibition of Dedication of Women in Temples Act

> It took one more year for me to obtain permission to introduce the bill in the legislative assembly. Then it was sent to the Scrutiny Committee where some useful corrections were made and it took proper shape. Even though I wanted to vanquish this demon, I did not have the requisite details to formulate a law. These were resolved in the Scrutiny Committee discussions. In this regard, I can never forgive the invaluable support rendered by the leader CVS Narasimha Raju Garu. Even though, I had deep knowledge of the evils of the devadasi system, I was a novice as far as intricate legal knowledge went.

Devadasi women were allotted lands for the services rendered to temples. In reality, only a few women had the registration in their names. Other lands remained in the name of the temple and only the income from the lands was given to devadasi women.

Even though the Indian Penal Code (IPC) sections 372, 373 clearly banned the dedication of young girls as devadasis to temples, the practice continued. Hence, a law was enacted to eradicate this practice completely. In this regard, the Mysore kingdom was a forerunner. Way back in 1909, they had realized the severity of the problem. But we struggled against the sanatana followers for 60 years.

Finally, in February 1929, the act was promulgated. The government ordered the district collectors to turn over the lands to the devadasi women and free them from the practice. Earlier, when I tried to bring in the Prevention of Child Marriage Act, there were criticisms from all over the country. But, in the effort to abolish the devadasi system, I found support from all sections of society.

The Devadasi Prevention Act was included as an amendment to the Hindu Endowment Act, which regulated the property owned by temples. The free lands were assigned to the devadasis. I did not know that some temples did not come under this purview. For example, temples with an income below ₹300 and those in Chennai were given exemptions. Similarly, I did not know that girls were bought or adopted and were dedicated after they attained 18 years of age.

I prepared a complementary resolution to fulfil my desire to eradicate the devadasi practice completely. However, the government wilfully created delays in accepting the resolution. The government also passed an order to suspend the implementation of the Devadasi Prohibition Act. The resolution brought forward by the government was to defer my resolution. I strongly opposed the move.

I spoke on the unfair means of government to put obstacles to implement a policy that it had accepted and passed in the assembly. I was deeply suspicious of the government's deferral order against its own policy.

However, it was not new for the assembly. For many years, there have been demands for such an Act. I knew about the central government's views on this issue following the objection raised at an international conference against the practice of dedication. In 1912, the issue was discussed in the British-run parliament: At that time, an order was passed to send a circular to all states. It was enough if sitting members paid heed to the circulars. All state governments had sent notices to abolish the devadasi practice. They had requested for a law prohibiting the practice. Had we accepted those, there would have been a different history. But no such thing happened. The British-run Parliament appointed a three-member committee consisting of Maneckji Dadabhoy, Mudholkar and Madge to examine the issue. That committee examined and recommended three different laws similar to the ones that I had presented. Then, the central government sent it for the perusal of the state governments.

Based on these opinions, on September 1913, a motion was brought forward. It was sent to the Scrutiny Committee in 1914. However, the World War broke out and it was deferred. Later, in 1922, Sir Harisingh Gaur moved the resolution in the Assembly and it was unanimously accepted. I would like to draw your attention to the fact that when there was discussion on the matter, Shiv Rao and Sir AB Patro supported the devadasi practice. However, the assembly set aside their remarks and adopted Gaur's resolution. Because of this, the dedication of girls was made a punishable offence under IPC 372 and 373.

I mentioned this only to indicate the support across the nation for the Devadasi Prohibition Act. In 1927, Ramdas Pantulu also brought a resolution on this matter and it was unanimously adopted. Later, the Law Minister advised that the resolution can be submitted for enactment. Many years earlier Mysore had enacted the law. The Bombay government was about to enact one. The Madras government enacted the law but through a deferral order put it in cold storage.

The law that I want to bring is gentle. Its aim is only to announce that the dedication of women is against the law. We can enact this under criminal law but that has been made inactive. The sanatanis opine that only girls below 12 years of age should be dedicated. However, those who are slaves of the devadasi practice do not obey the criminal laws. They have escaped by citing religious norms. That is, instead of dedicating girls at 12, they escape the clutches of law by dedicating them at 18. This is because this law did not put the onus of responsibility on the temples or the guardians. My aim is to prevent the dedication. There's another aspect to this issue. It is about the right of the devadasi woman to marry. The Hindu Religious Act prohibits devadasis from entering into conjugal life through marriage. Devadasis who marry are forced to return the temple land. The law that I propose allows the devadasi to marry even after dedication. The government need not worry about a public backlash. It was enacted several years back in Mysore. The Mysore kingdom has banned the practice of performing gajja puja as a prelude to dedication. In this respect, the Mysore government is a leader by example. Our government also accepts the fact that dedication ruins the lives of girls. There is no justification in deferring it after accepting it in principle. The Devadasi Prohibition Act only refers to free land received by devadasis. This does not involve religion. It is deliberate and planned to force women into amoral lives. Hence, there is no justification in delaying it further. So, the member who has opposed my bill has to recall his petition and forward mine to the Scrutiny Committee.

On 5 November 1927, the Vice President of Justice Party, M Krishnan Nair extended wholehearted support to the motion of prevention of dedications. He is now in the ruling party. Even so, he has proposed to recall the deferral order. Is this change brought about because Justice Party is in power? Or is it because of the death of the Panagal ruler? Only people can judge. It is a great loss that my good friend, the Panagal ruler who strengthened my conviction and resolve is not with us.

In 1929, the Madras Act was passed in the Madras Assembly. 'In all temples, devadasis or dancing girls who were given free land in exchange of the services for which they were appointed. This Act gives them ownership of the land. By this order, they are no longer required to perform any services at the temples.' This Act was concluded only after the 31st enactment of Law brought out in 1947. Only after that was the devadasi practice completely abolished.

Glossary

Pitti Thiagarayar was one of the founders and considered the Father of the Justice Party. He was also one of the 'Big Three' of the Dravidian movement. In 1881, he started the Madras Native Association, which was later renamed as Madras Mahajana Sabha. The locality T Nagar in Chennai is named after him.

T M Nair: Dr Tarawad Madhavan Nair was one the founding members of the Dravidian movement. He studied in England and worked as an ENT specialist there. In 1904, he was selected as Commissioner of Madras Municipal Corporation and served in that capacity for 12 years. (This post is now called Ward Councillor.)

C Natesan is among the three important founders of the Dravidian movement. He coined the term 'Dravidar' to refer to Tamil, Malayali, Telugu and Kannada people. In 1912, he started the Dravidian Association of Madras, Later, Pitti Thiagarayar gave it a political framework and it emerged as the Justice Party. In 1920, he contested in the general elections and won the largest number of votes in the Chennai area, He served as MLA for two terms from 1920-1926 and 1935-1937.

Sathyavani Muthu was the Social Welfare Minister when the Dravida Munnetra Kazhagam (DMK) was formed for the first time under the leadership of Arignar Annadurai. She belongs to the Scheduled Caste community. She published the magazine *Annai.*

Moovalur Singaravelu Pandithar was the Tamil pundit who taught Moovalurar. He was instrumental in changing the nomenclature of the Devadasi Community from Nagapasathar to Isai Vellalar.

E V Ramasamy Naicker was popularly known as Thanthai Periyar. He was a freedom fighter and was the main root of the Dravidian movement. He was an atheist and severely criticized the customs and norms that were blindly accepted by people. He was a political and social reformer and conducted many self-respect marriages. He was editor of *Kudiarasu* and *Viduthalai* magazines, and a political leader who did not take part in election politics.

C Rajagopalachari, popularly known as Rajaji or Mootharignar, was a lawyer and freedom fighter. He was the last Governor-General of India and also served in various capacities in the state and the central governments. He was an accomplished writer and translator.

Thiru Vi Ka was a popular reference to Thiruvarur Kalyanasundaram Mudaliar. He was a freedom fighter and started the Labour Union. He was the Editor of *Dravidan* and *Navashakti* magazines. He was an influential public speaker and known as 'Tamil Thendral' for his oratory prowess.

Karaikudi Chinnayya Pillai was a well-known musician and leader of the Congress Party.

Kumbakonam Pantulu Iyer was a prominent leader of the Congress Party.

Koranadu Thillai Ammal was a musician and performer. She was one of the prominent persons, who walked out of the devadasi system.

Chidambaram Janakathammal led staunch protests against the devadasi system and the practice of dedication of young girls to temples. She was a musician and performing artist.

Thiruvavaduthurai Rajarathinam Pillai was a well-known Nagaswaram player and known by the honorific, 'Nagaswara Chakravarthi.'

Varadarajulu Naidu was a journalist and freedom fighter. He worked closely with Thanthai Periyar. He contested the general elections in 1952 and became an MLA.

S Ramanathan was known as 'Periyar's right hand man' and the 'brain of the self-respect movement.' When Periyar left the Congress Party, he walked out as well. Later, in 1937, he contested and won as the candidate of the Congress Party and served as the Minister of Publicity.

N Dhandapani Pillai was a musician and a leader of the Congress Party.

S V Lingam was instrumental in shaping the Dravidian Movement. He introduced and brought many important people into its fold.

K Thirunavukkarasu is a senior journalist and well-known researcher on the Dravidian movement. He is the author of works such as *Roots of Dravidian Movement, Pillars of Dravidian Movement* and *History of the Justice Party.*

Karaikudi Ramasubbiah was a prominent member of the Dravidian movement.

Thanjavur K Natarajan was a prominent member of the Congress Party.

Sirkazhi T N Subbiah Pillai was a renowned Nagaswaram player.

Arumugam Chettiar provided valuable information about Moovalurar to the author of this book. He studied in the *pyol* school where she used to teach music. He conducted daily discourses on *Periyapuranam* in the local temple.

Kandasamy Thevar was a renowned sculptor whose sculptures can be seen in the Mayiladuthurai Mayuranatha swamy temple.

Siddakadu Meenakshisundaram was a retired teacher, who provided first-hand information about Moovalurar to the author of this book.

Mayuramani Chinnayya Pillai was a prominent leader of the Congress Party.

Yamuna Boorana Thilakamma was the chairperson of the Fallen Sisters Home in Andhra Pradesh.

Marudur Kandasamy Pillai was a musician and a Congress leader.

Ratinam was the Adi Dravida woman employed by Moovalurar in response to Gandhiji's call for social inclusion.

Mirasudar was a term used to refer to local landlords.

Va Ve Subramaniam Iyer was a Barrister at Law from London. He belonged to a group of revolutionary freedom fighters and was exiled in Pondicherry along with Bharathiyar and V O Chidambaram.

Samy Chidambaran was a school teacher and an ardent follower of Periyar.

Kuthoosi Gurusamy belonged to the intellectual group of the Dravidian movement. He was editor of English magazine, *Revolt.*

K V Azhagarsamy was known as 'Anja Nenjar' or braveheart. He was brought into the party by S V Lingam.

M Singaravelan was the first prominent Communist leader in Tamil Nadu. He was a trade unionist and initiated the practice of celebrating May Day as Labour Day.

P Jeevanandam was a well-known leader of the Communist Party.

Kunjitham was an educationist. Hailing from the devadasi community, she broke the shackles of tradition through education. Hers was the first self-respect marriage. She was the first editor to publish Bharathidasan's poetry.

Maragathavalli was editor of the magazine, *Madhar Marumanam* (Women's Remarriage).

Neelavathi married Ramasubramaniam Chettiar through an inter-caste marriage. She was editor of the magazine *Rajyalakshmi.* She conducted many remarriages of widows. She did not take up any post in the cabinet even when Kamarajar offered.

Dr Muthulakshmi Reddy was among the first women doctors and the first woman MLA. She was instrumental in getting the Acts prohibiting the devadasi system and child marriage.

Sathyamurthy was a freedom fighter. He opposed the abolition of the devadasi system.

Dharmambal was a Siddha doctor specialized in dermatology, who belonged to the Self-Respect Movement. She courted arrest during the anti-Hindi protest. The Tamil Nadu government has instituted a Widow Remarriage Assistance Scheme in her name.

T K Sreenivasan was a writer and journalist. He was fondly referred as the 'Philosopher' in Dravidian Movement circles.

Poovalur A Ponnambalam was a brilliant orator and spoke at a very fast pace. He was popularly known as 'Boat Mail Ponnambalam' after the Boat Mail Express. He was a founding member of the Self-Respect Movement.

A S Arunachalam was a noted public speaker and a founding member of the Self-Respect Movement.

Pattammal Balasundaram was a member of the Self-Respect Movement and went to jail during the anti-Hindi agitation.

Malrmugathu Ammaiyar was a reformist and prominent member of the Self-Respect Movement. She courted arrest during the anti-Hindi protests.

Seethammal was the daughter-in-law of Pattammal. She was also a prominent member of the Self-Respect Movement, who went to jail during the anti-Hindi imposition protests.

Pudumai Penn Thittam is a scheme launched by the Tamil Nadu government to help girls achieve their educational aspirations. It has been named after Moovalurar.

Samachir Kalvi Thittam is an educational scheme initiated by the Government of Tamil Nadu to ensure a uniform syllabus in government schools across the state.

Thandiyam Pidithal: *Thandiyam* means pestle. It is considered a phallic symbol to announce the maturing of a devadasi girl.

Gajja Puja: The term *gajja* means anklets. The tying of the anklets around the young devadasi girl's ankles not only marks her initiation into a life of dance and music but also as a dedicated girl who belongs to the temple.

Annapurani and Rathinasabapathy: Their marriage was a prominent inter-caste marriage conducted under the banner of the Self-Respect Movement.

Kanakasabhai Nadar was a well-educated and affluent merchant. He was a prominent member of the Justice Party.

Meenambal Vellaithambi is the daughter-in-law of Kanakasabhai Nadar and provided valuable first-hand information to the author of this book.

Kaliyamurthy also provided valuable first-hand information to the author of this book.

D V Narayanasamy was a theatre artist and film actor. He was a functionary in the Self-Respect Movement and was a very articulate orator.

Rajammal was a prominent member of the Self-Respect Movement.